SUPER EASY SONGBOOK

CHRISTMAS CAROLS

Hkac

D1452219

ISBN 978-1-5400-2913-3

HAL•LEONARD®

Visit Hal Leonard Online at
www.halleonard.com

Contact Us:
Hal Leonard
7777 West Bluemound Road
Milwaukee, WI 53213
Email: info@halleonard.com

In Europe contact:
Hal Leonard Europe Limited
Distribution Centre, Newmarket Road
Bury St Edmunds, Suffolk, IP33 3YB
Email: info@halleonardeurope.com

In Australia contact:
Hal Leonard Australia Pty. Ltd.
4 Lentara Court
Cheltenham, Victoria, 3192 Australia
Email: info@halleonard.com.au

NOV -- 2018

Welcome to the *Super Easy Songbook* series!

This unique collection will help you play your favorite songs quickly and easily. Here's how it works:

- Play the simplified melody with your right hand. Letter names appear inside each note to assist you.

- There are no key signatures to worry about! If a sharp ♯ or flat ♭ is needed, it is shown beside the note each time.

- There are no page turns, so your hands never have to leave the keyboard.

- If two notes are connected by a tie ⌣, hold the first note for the combined number of beats. (The second note does not show a letter name since it is not re-struck.)

- Add basic chords with your left hand using the provided keyboard diagrams. Chord voicings have been carefully chosen to minimize hand movement.

- The left-hand rhythm is up to you, and chord notes can be played together or separately. Be creative!

- If the chords sound muddy, move your left hand an octave* higher. If this gets in the way of playing the melody, move your right hand an octave higher as well.

  An octave spans eight notes. If your starting note is C, the next C to the right is an octave higher.

─────────────── ALSO AVAILABLE ───────────────

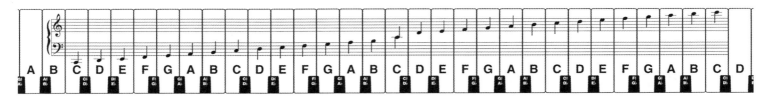

Hal Leonard Student Keyboard Guide HL00296039

Key Stickers HL00100016

Angels from the Realms of Glory

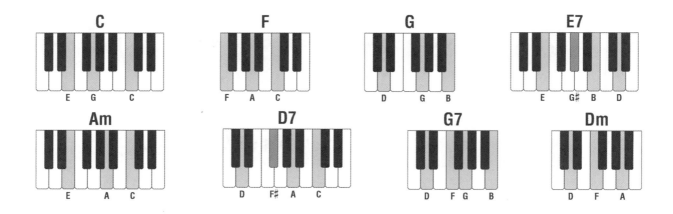

Words by James Montgomery
Music by Henry T. Smart

Moderately

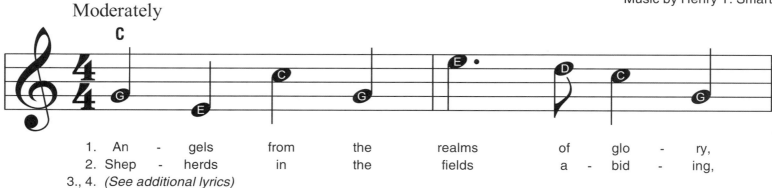

1. An - gels   from   the   realms   of   glo - ry,
2. Shep - herds   in   the   fields   a - bid - ing,
3., 4. *(See additional lyrics)*

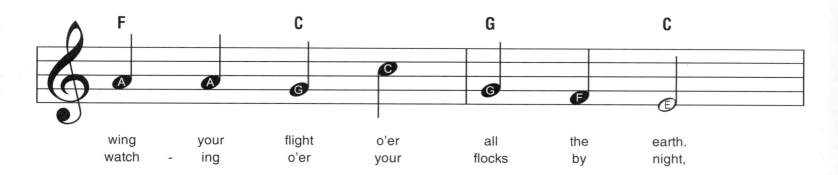

wing   your   flight   o'er   all   the   earth.
watch - ing   o'er   your   flocks   by   night,

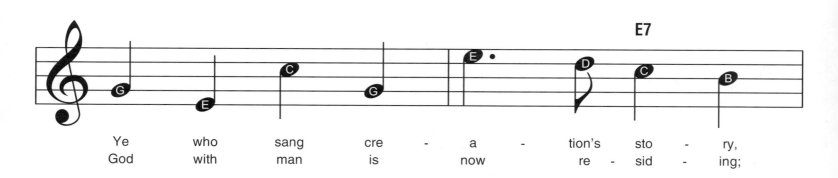

Ye   who   sang   cre - a - tion's   sto - ry,
God   with   man   is   now   re - sid - ing;

7

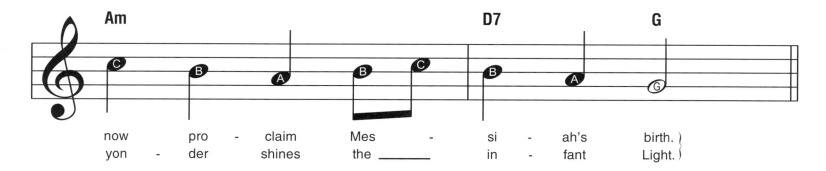

Refrain

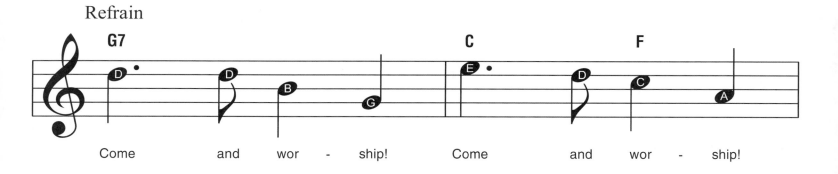

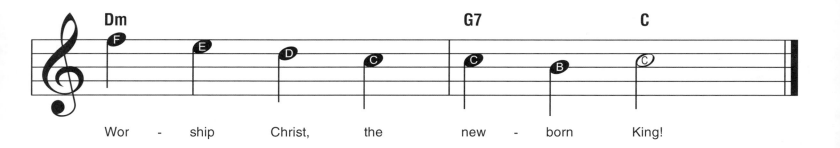

Additional Lyrics

3. Sages, leave your contemplations,
   Brighter visions beam afar.
   Seek the great desire of nations,
   Ye have seen His natal star.
   Refrain

4. Saints before the altar bending,
   Watching long in hope and fear,
   Suddenly the Lord, descending,
   In His temple shall appear.
   Refrain

Angels We Have Heard on High

 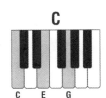 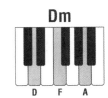 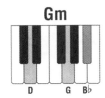 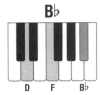

Traditional French Carol
Translated by James Chadwick

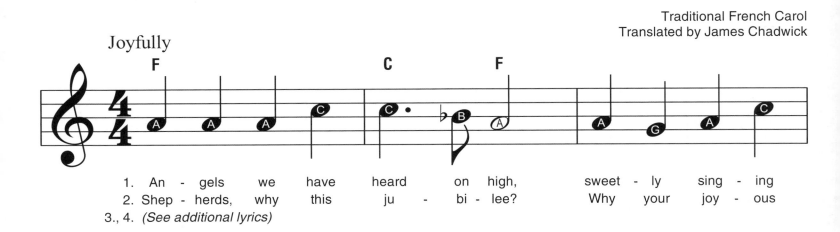

1. An - gels we have heard on high, sweet - ly sing - ing
2. Shep - herds, why this ju - bi - lee? Why your joy - ous
3., 4. *(See additional lyrics)*

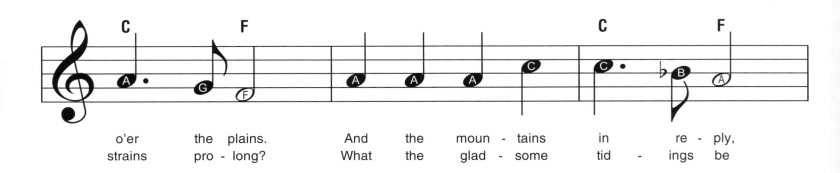

o'er the plains. And the moun - tains in re - ply,
strains pro - long? What the glad - some tid - ings be

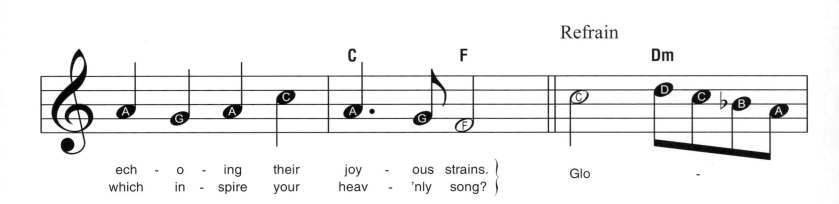

ech - o - ing their joy - ous strains. } Glo -
which in - spire your heav - 'nly song? }

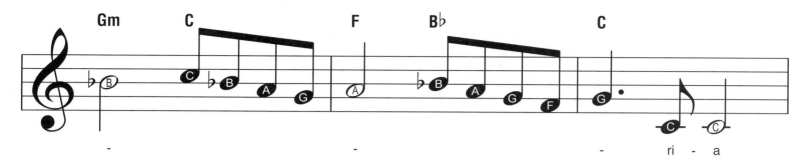

\- - - ri - a

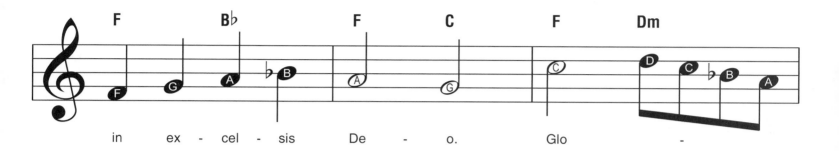

in ex - cel - sis De - o. Glo -

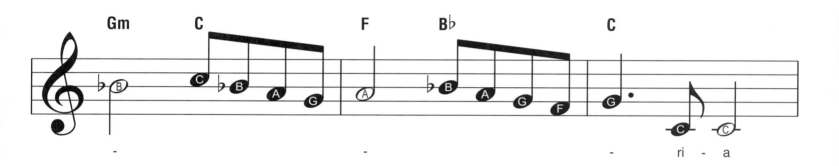

\- - - ri - a

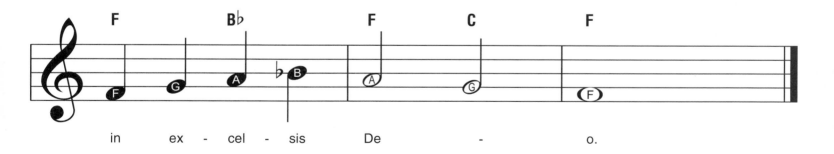

in ex - cel - sis De - o.

Additional Lyrics

3. Come to Bethlehem and see
   Him whose birth the angels sing.
   Come adore on bended knee
   Christ, the Lord, the newborn King.
   Refrain

4. See within a manger laid
   Jesus, Lord of heav'n and earth.
   Mary, Joseph, lend your aid,
   With us sing our Savior's birth.
   Refrain

As with Gladness Men of Old

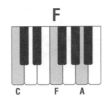 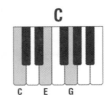 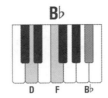

Words by William Chatterton Dix
Music by Conrad Kocher

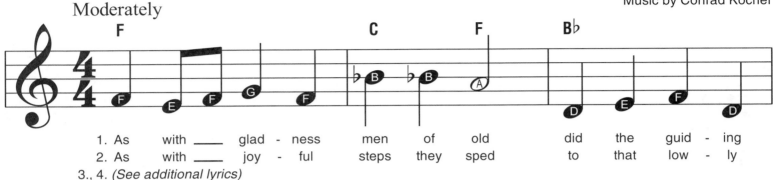

1. As with _____ glad - ness men of old did the guid - ing
2. As with _____ joy - ful steps they sped to that low - ly

3., 4. *(See additional lyrics)*

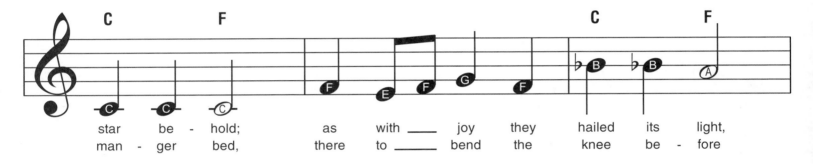

star be - hold; as with _____ joy they hailed its light,
man - ger bed, there to _____ bend the knee be - fore

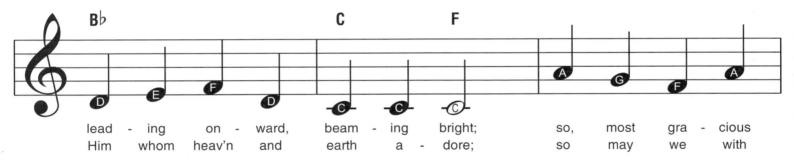

lead - ing on - ward, beam - ing bright; so, most gra - cious
Him whom heav'n and earth a - dore; so may we with

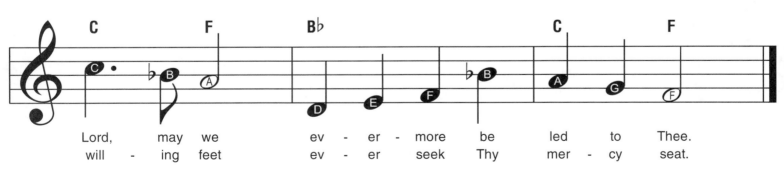

Lord, may we ev - er - more be led to Thee.
will - ing feet ev - er seek Thy mer - cy seat.

Additional Lyrics

3. As they offered gifts most rare
   At that manger rude and bare,
   So may we with holy joy,
   Pure and free from sin's alloy,
   All our costliest treasures bring,
   Christ, to Thee, our heav'nly King.

4. Holy Jesus, ev'ry day
   Keep us in the narrow way;
   And when earthly things are past,
   Bring our ransomed souls at last
   Where they need no star to guide,
   Where no clouds Thy glory hide.

Auld Lang Syne

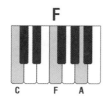 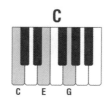 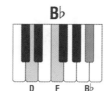  

Words by Robert Burns
Traditional Scottish Melody

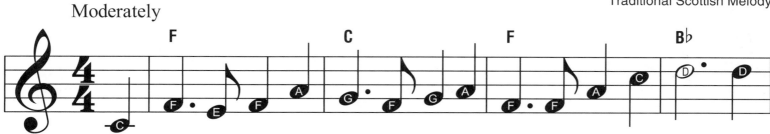

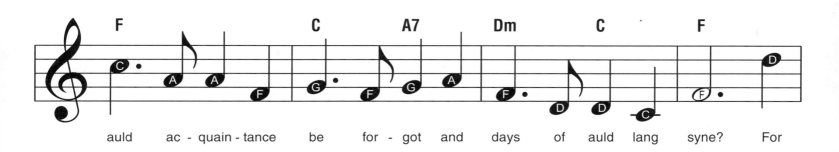

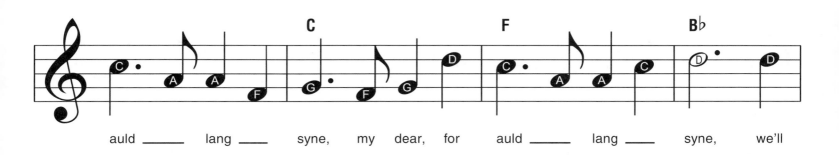

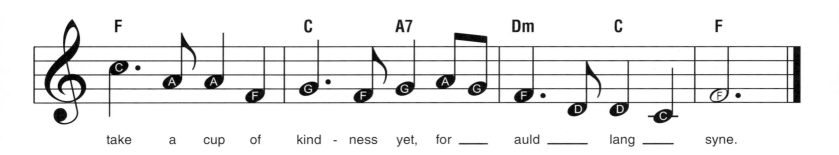

Away in a Manger

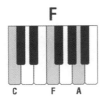 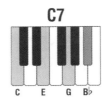 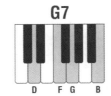

Words by John T. McFarland (v.3)
Music by William J. Kirkpatrick

A - way in a _____ man - ger, no _____ crib for a
The cat - tle are _____ low - ing; the _____ Ba - by a -
Be near me, Lord _____ Je - sus; I _____ ask Thee to

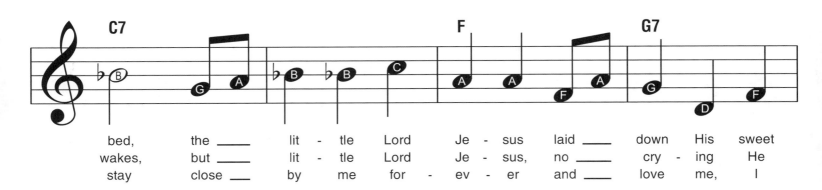

bed, the _____ lit - tle Lord Je - sus laid _____ down His sweet
wakes, but _____ lit - tle Lord Je - sus, no _____ cry - ing He
stay close _____ by me for - ev - er and _____ love me, I

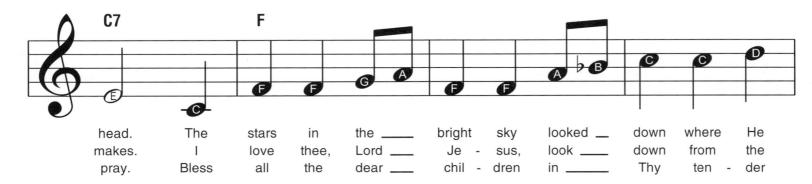

head. The stars in the _____ bright sky looked _ down where He
makes. I love thee, Lord _____ Je - sus, look _____ down from the
pray. Bless all the dear _____ chil - dren in _____ Thy ten - der

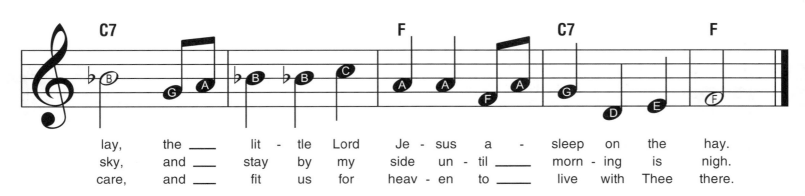

lay, the _____ lit - tle Lord Je - sus a - sleep on the hay.
sky, and _____ stay by my side un - til _____ morn - ing is nigh.
care, and _____ fit us for heav - en to _____ live with Thee there.

Away in a Manger

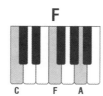
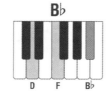
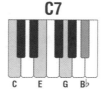

Words by John T. McFarland (v.3)
Music by James R. Murray

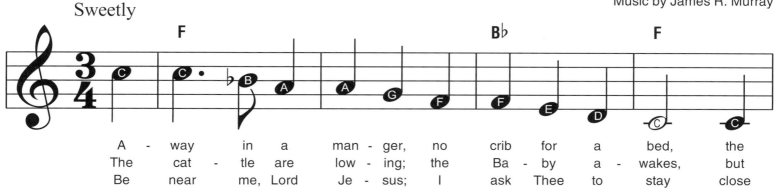

A - way in a man - ger, no crib for a bed, the
The cat - tle are low - ing; the Ba - by a - wakes, but
Be near me, Lord Je - sus; I ask Thee to stay close

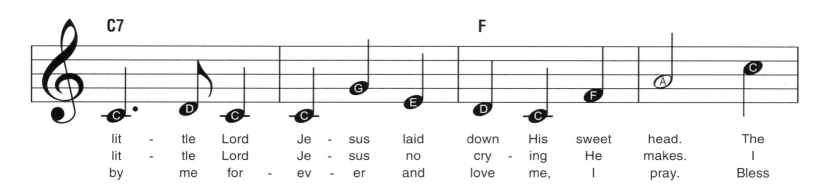

lit - tle Lord Je - sus laid down His sweet head. The
lit - tle Lord Je - sus no cry - ing He makes. I
by me for - ev - er and love me, I pray. Bless

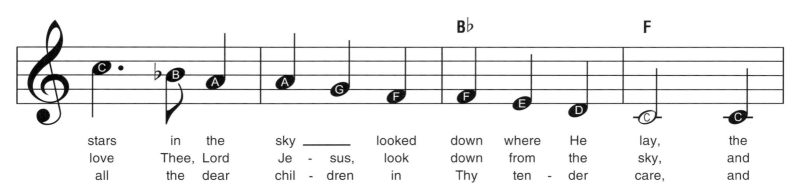

stars in the sky _____ looked down where He lay, the
love Thee, Lord Je - sus, look down from the sky, and
all the dear chil - dren in Thy ten - der care, and

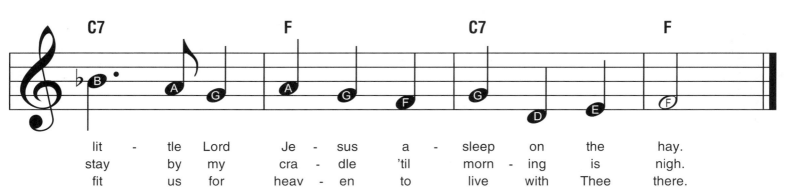

lit - tle Lord Je - sus a - sleep on the hay.
stay by my cra - dle 'til morn - ing is nigh.
fit us for heav - en to live with Thee there.

The Birthday of a King

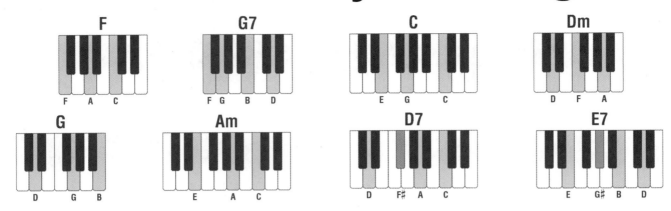

Words and Music by
William H. Neidlinger

Moderately

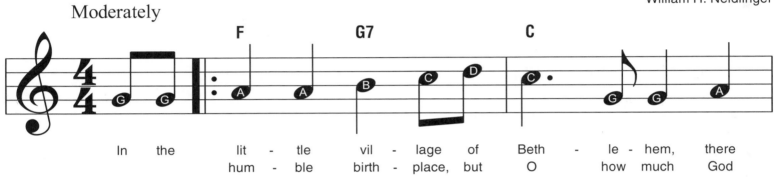

In the lit - tle vil - lage of Beth - le - hem, there
hum - ble birth - place, but O how much there God

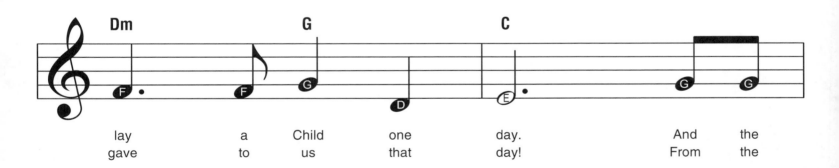

lay a Child one day. And the
gave to us one that day! From the

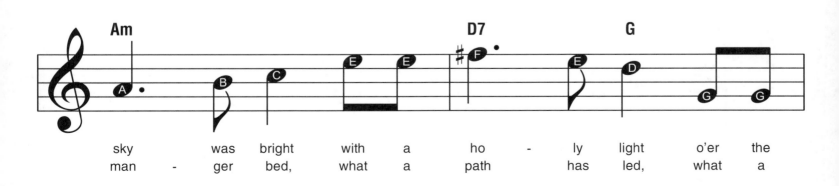

sky was bright with a ho - ly light o'er the
man - ger bed, what a path has led, what a

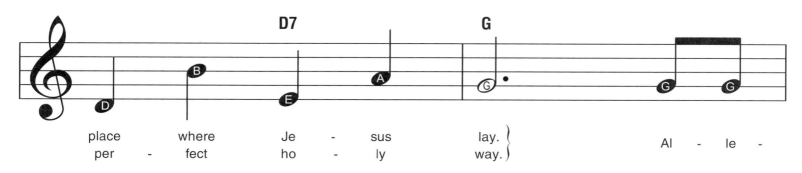

place where Je - sus lay. }
per - fect ho - ly way. }
Al - le -

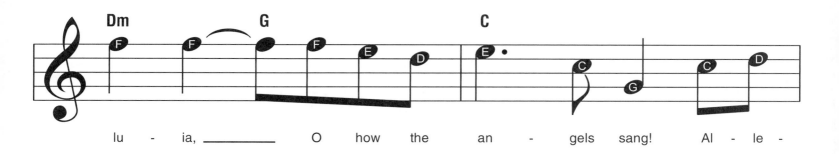

lu - ia, _____ O how the an - gels sang! Al - le -

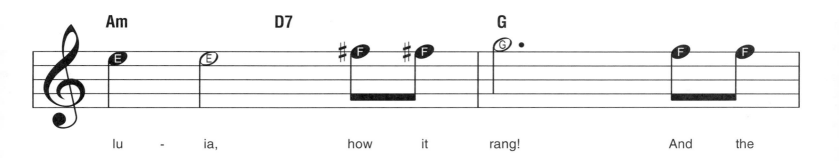

lu - ia, how it rang! And the

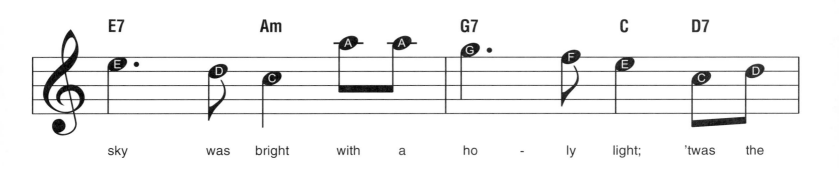

sky was bright with a ho - ly light; 'twas the

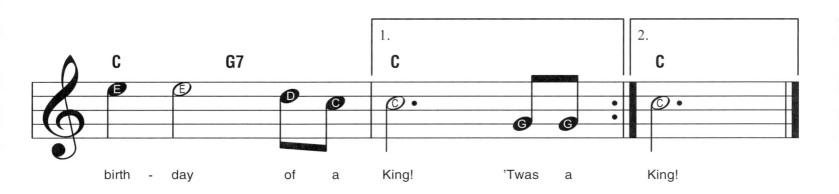

birth - day of a King! 'Twas a King!

Bring a Torch, Jeannette, Isabella

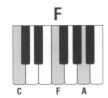 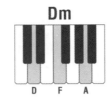 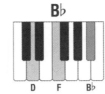 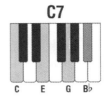

17th Century French Provençal Carol

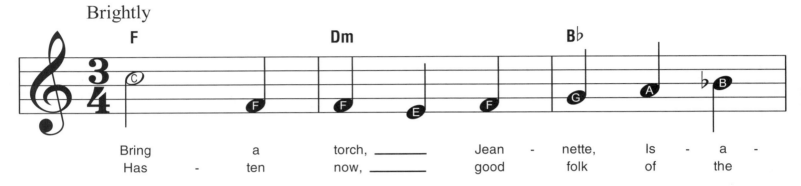

Bring a torch, _____ Jean - nette, Is - a -
Has - ten now, _____ good folk of the

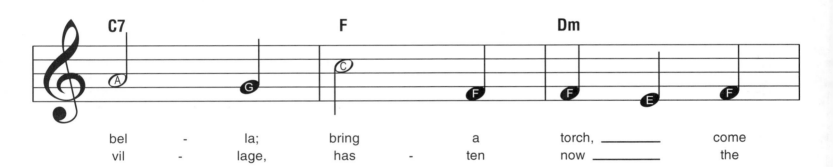

bel - la; bring a torch, _____ come
vil - lage, bring has - ten now _____ the

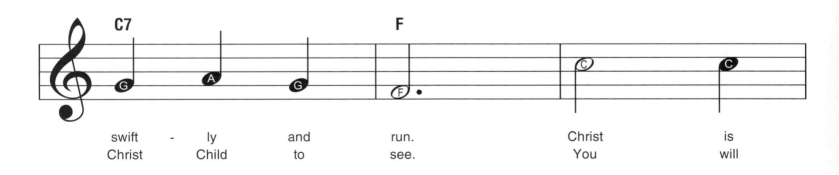

swift - ly and run. Christ is
Christ Child to see. You will

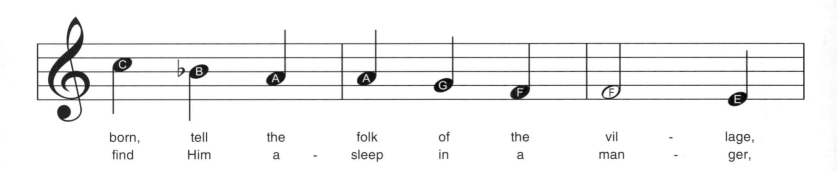

born, tell the folk of the vil - lage,
find Him a - sleep in a man - ger,

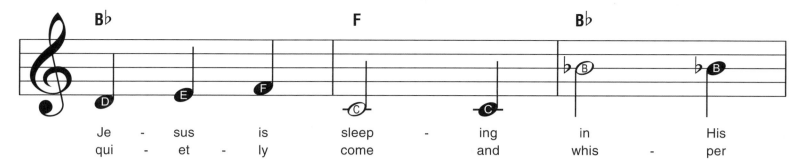

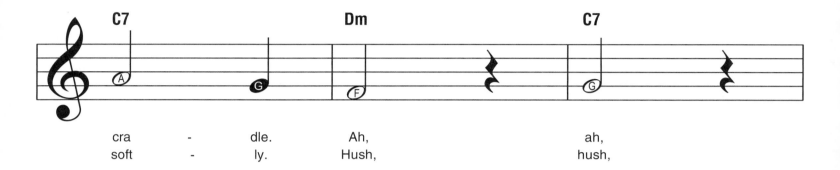

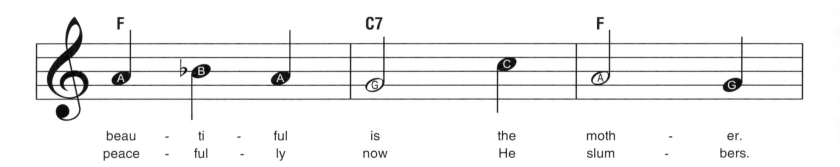

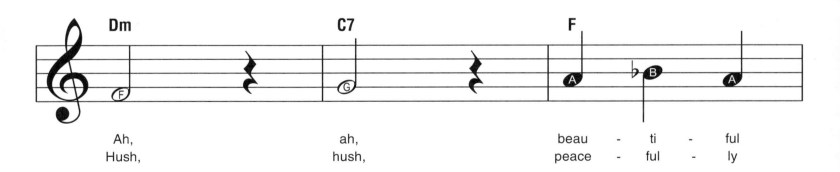

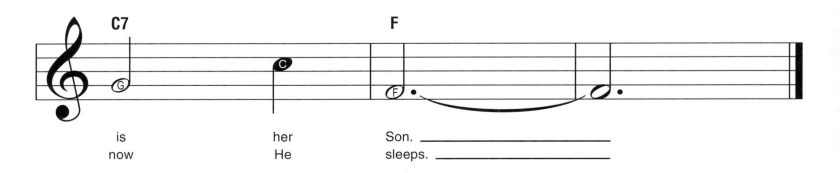

A Child Is Born in Bethlehem

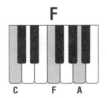 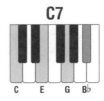 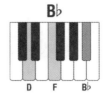 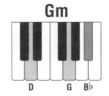

14th-Century Latin Text adapted by
Nicolai F.S. Grundtvig
Traditional Danish Melody

Joyfully

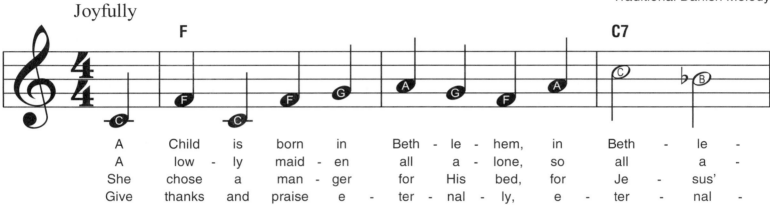

A Child is born in Beth - le - hem, in Beth - le -
A low - ly maid - en all a - lone, so all a -
She chose a man - ger for His bed, for Je - sus'
Give thanks and praise e - ter - nal - ly, e - ter - nal -

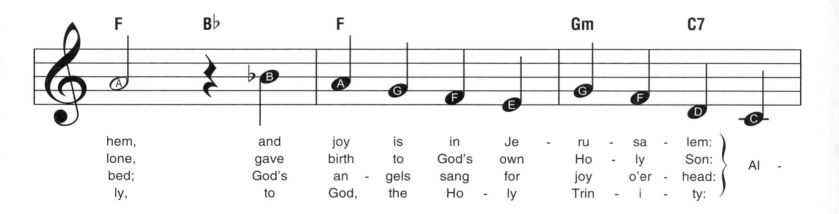

hem,   and joy is in Je - ru - sa - lem:
lone,   gave birth to God's own Ho - ly Son: } Al -
bed;   God's an - gels sang for joy o'er - head:
ly,   to God, the Ho - ly Trin - i - ty:

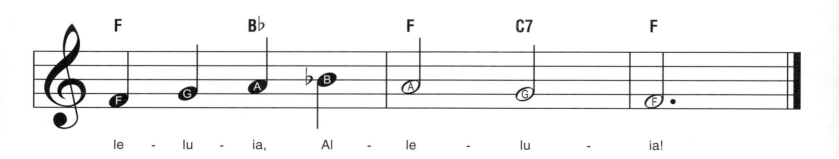

le - lu - ia, Al - le - lu - ia!

Christ Was Born on Christmas Day

Traditional

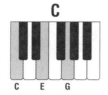
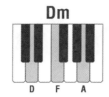
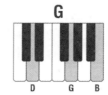
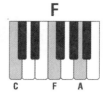

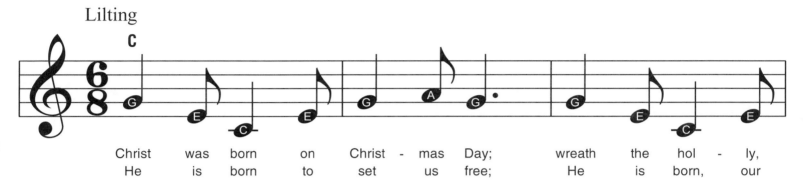

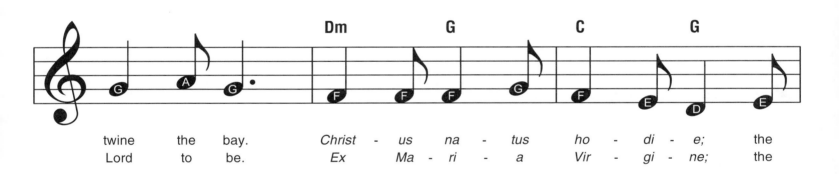

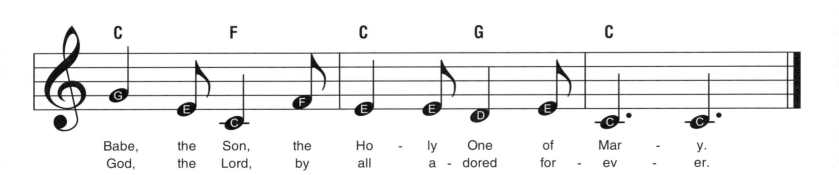

Come, Thou Long-Expected Jesus

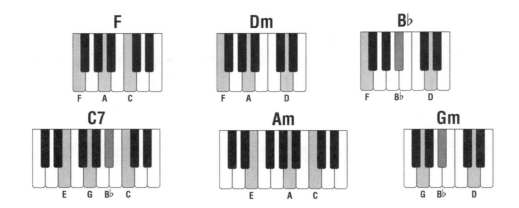

Words by Charles Wesley
Music by Rowland Hugh Prichard

Moderately fast

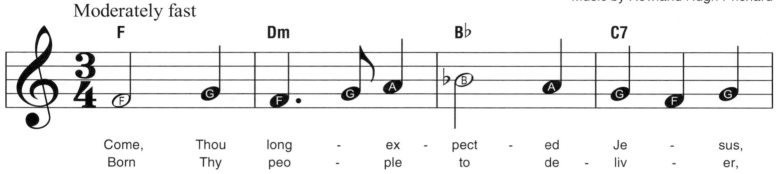

Come, Thou long - ex - pect - ed Je - sus,
Born Thy peo - ple to de - liv - er,

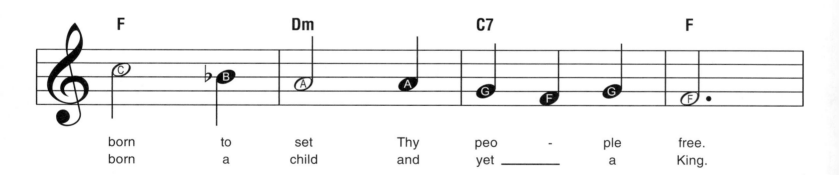

born to set Thy peo - ple free.
born a child and yet _____ a King.

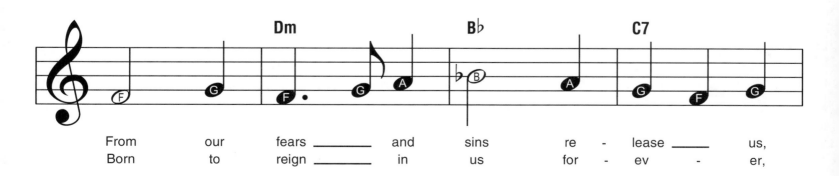

From our fears _____ and sins re - lease _____ us,
Born to reign _____ in us for - ev - er,

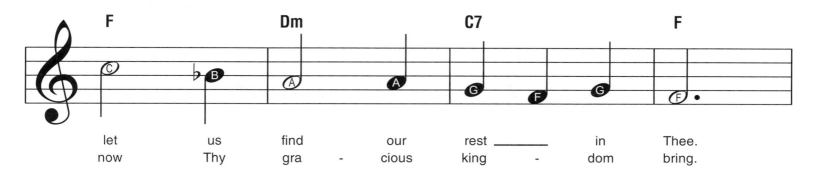

let us find our rest _____ in Thee.
now Thy gra - cious king - dom bring.

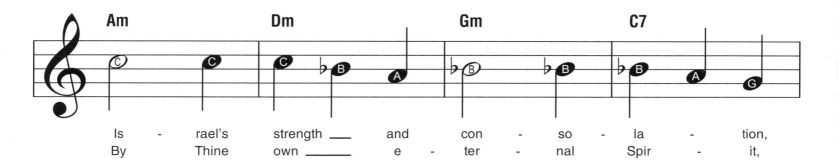

Is - rael's strength ___ and con - so - la - tion,
By Thine own _____ e - ter - nal Spir - it,

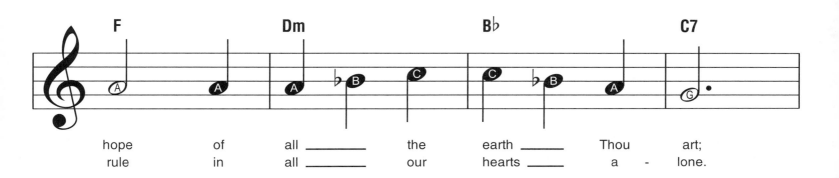

hope of all _____ the earth _____ Thou art;
rule in all _____ our hearts _____ a - lone.

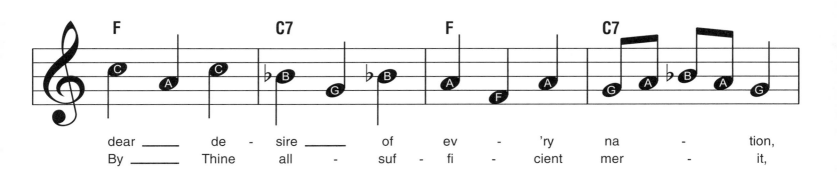

dear _____ de - sire _____ of ev - 'ry na - tion,
By _____ Thine all - suf - fi - cient mer - it,

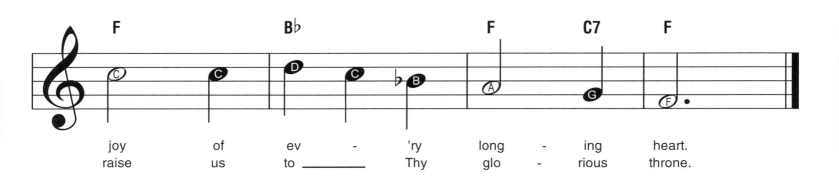

joy of ev - 'ry long - ing heart.
raise us to _____ Thy glo - rious throne.

Coventry Carol

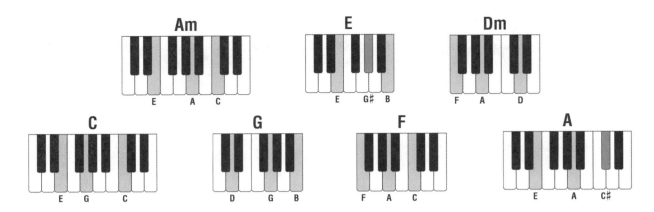

Words by Robert Croo
Traditional English Melody

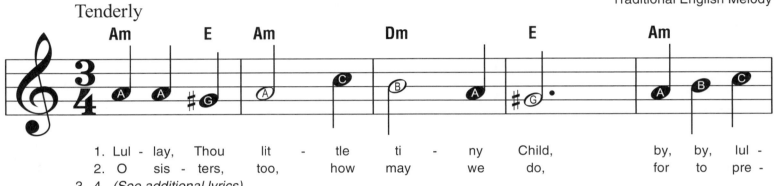

1. Lul - lay, Thou lit - tle ti - ny Child, by, by, lul -
2. O sis - ters, too, how may we do, for to pre -
3., 4. (See additional lyrics)

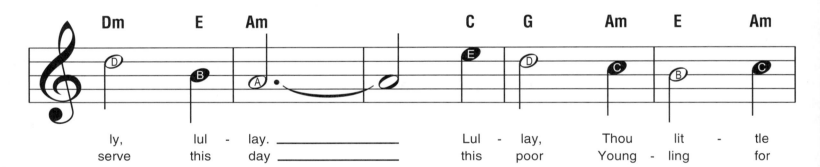

ly, lul - lay. _____ Lul - lay, Thou lit - tle
serve this day _____ this poor Young - ling for

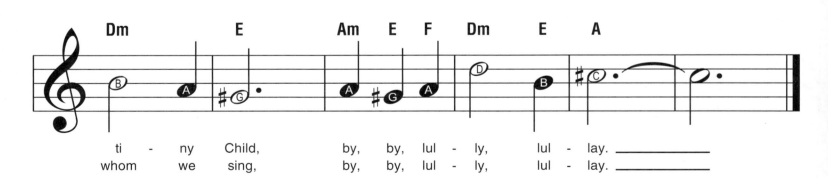

ti - ny Child, by, by, lul - ly, lul - lay. _____
whom we sing, by, by, lul - ly, lul - lay. _____

Additional Lyrics

3. Herod the king, in his raging,
   Charged he hath this day
   His men of might, in his own sight,
   All young children to slay.

4. That woe is me, poor Child, for Thee!
   And ever morn and day,
   For Thy parting neither say nor sing,
   By, by, lully, lullay.

The Friendly Beasts

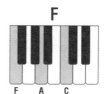 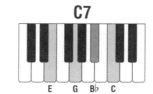 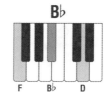

Traditional English Carol

Tenderly

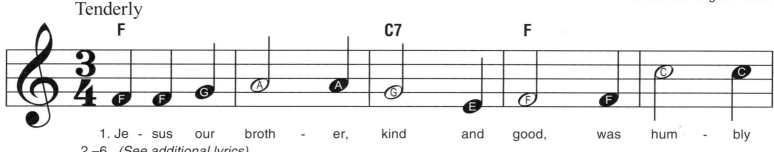

1. Je - sus our broth - er, kind and good, was hum - bly
2.–6. *(See additional lyrics)*

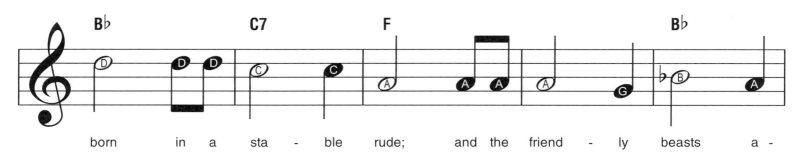

born in a sta - ble rude; and the friend - ly beasts a -

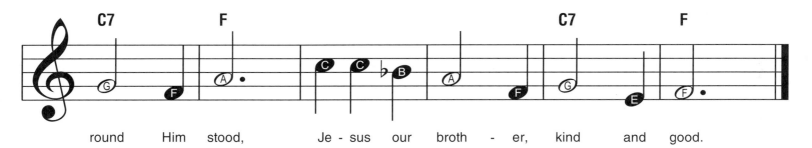

round Him stood, Je - sus our broth - er, kind and good.

Additional Lyrics

2. "I," said the donkey, shaggy and brown,
   "I carried His mother up hill and down.
   I carried His mother to Bethlehem town."
   "I," said the donkey, shaggy and brown.

3. "I," said the cow, all white and red,
   "I gave Him my manger for His bed.
   I gave Him my hay to pillow His head."
   "I," said the cow, all white and red.

4. "I," said the sheep with the curly horn,
   "I gave Him my wool for His blanket warm.
   He wore my coat on Christmas morn."
   "I," said the sheep with the curly horn.

5. "I," said the dove from the rafters high,
   "I cooed Him to sleep that He would not cry.
   We cooed Him to sleep, my mate and I."
   "I," said the dove from the rafters high.

6. Thus every beast, by some good spell,
   In the stable dark was glad to tell
   Of the gift he gave Emmanuel,
   The gift he gave Emmanuel.

Dance of the Sugar Plum Fairy

from THE NUTCRACKER SUITE, OP. 71A

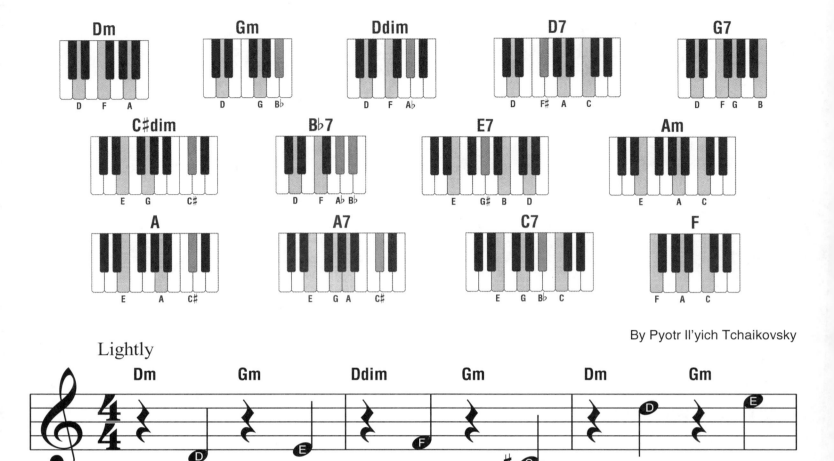

By Pyotr Il'yich Tchaikovsky

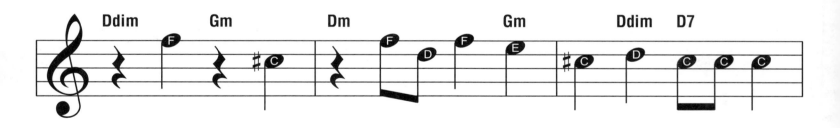

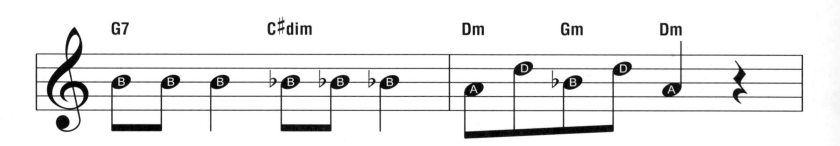

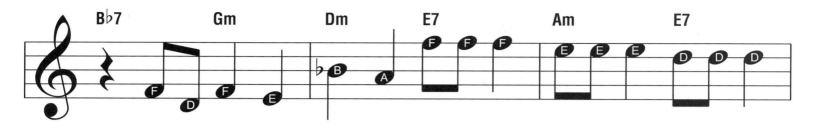

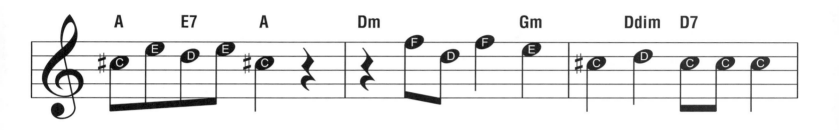

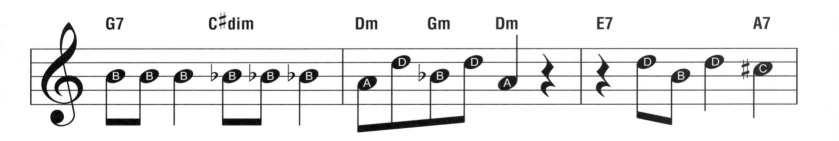

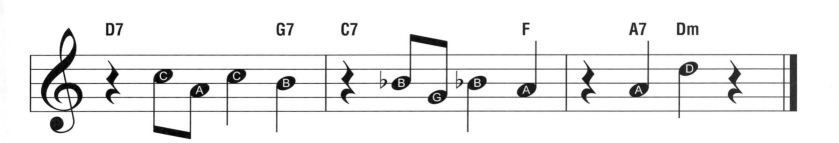

Deck the Hall

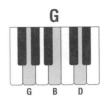  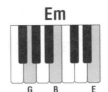 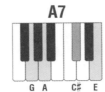 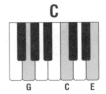

Traditional Welsh Carol

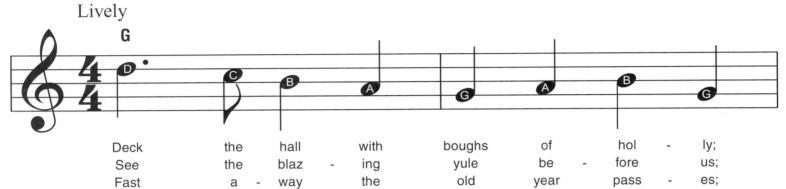

Deck the hall with boughs of hol - ly;
See the blaz - ing yule be - fore us;
Fast a - way the old year pass - es;

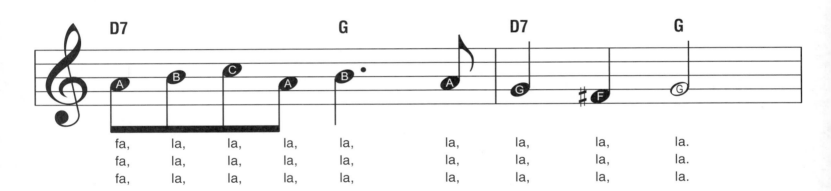

fa, la, la, la, la, la, la, la, la.
fa, la, la, la, la, la, la, la, la.
fa, la, la, la, la, la, la, la, la.

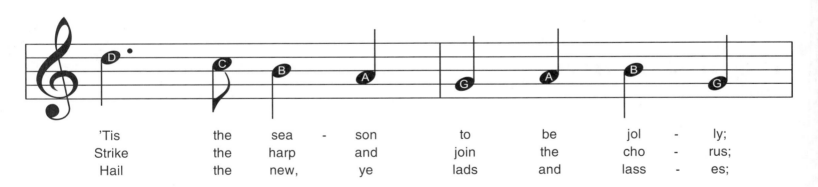

'Tis the sea - son to be jol - ly;
Strike the harp and join the cho - rus;
Hail the new, ye lads and lass - es;

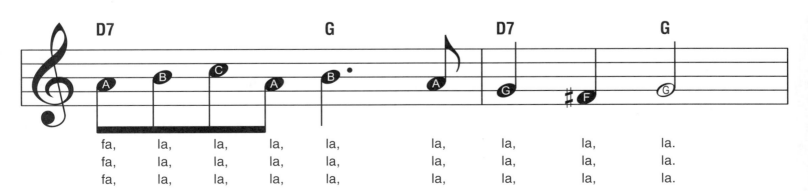

fa, la, la, la, la, la, la, la, la.
fa, la, la, la, la, la, la, la, la.
fa, la, la, la, la, la, la, la, la.

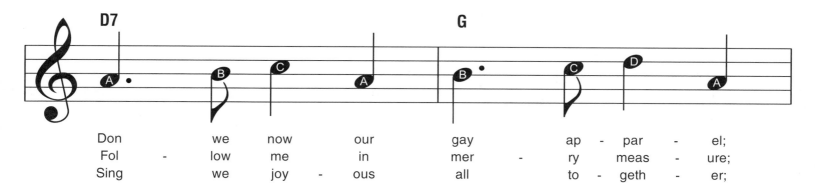

Don we now our gay ap - par - el;
Fol - low me in mer - ry meas - ure;
Sing we joy - ous all to - geth - er;

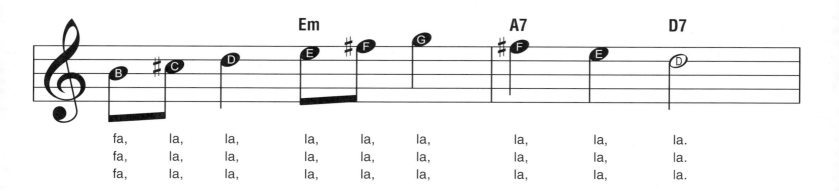

fa, la, la, la, la, la, la, la, la.
fa, la, la, la, la, la, la, la, la.
fa, la, la, la, la, la, la, la, la.

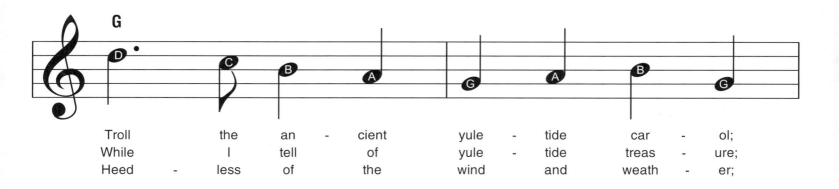

Troll the an - cient yule - tide car - ol;
While I tell of yule - tide treas - ure;
Heed - less of the wind and weath - er;

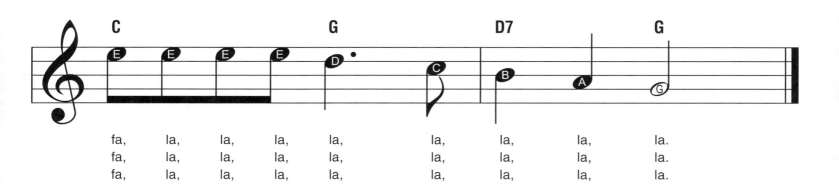

fa, la, la, la, la, la, la, la, la.
fa, la, la, la, la, la, la, la, la.
fa, la, la, la, la, la, la, la, la.

Ding Dong! Merrily on High!

F
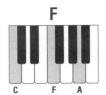

B♭
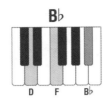

C7
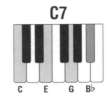

Dm
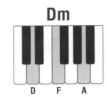

G7
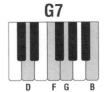

French Carol

Joyfully

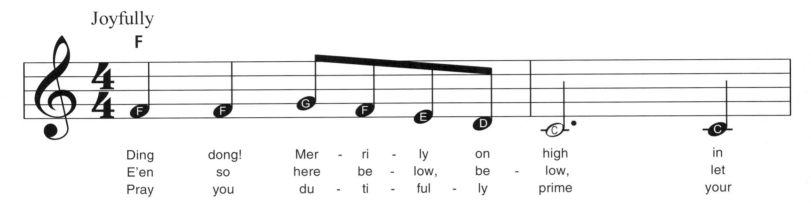

Ding dong! Mer - ri - ly on high in
E'en so here be - low, be - low, let
Pray you du - ti - ful - ly prime your

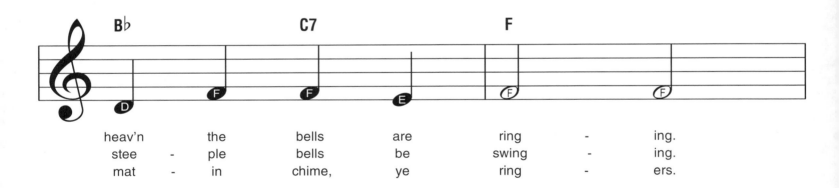

heav'n the bells are ring - ing.
stee - ple bells be swing - ing.
mat - in chime, ye ring - ers.

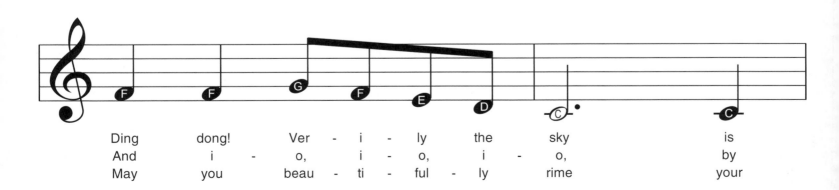

Ding dong! Ver - i - ly the sky is
And i - o, i - o, i - o, by
May you beau - ti - ful - ly rime your

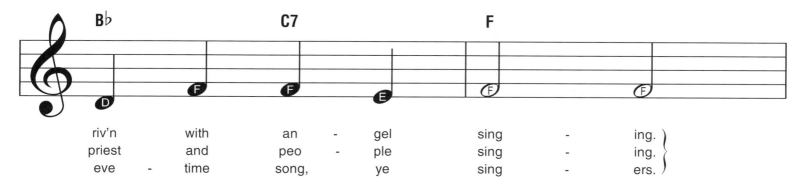

riv'n with an - gel sing - ing.
priest and peo - ple sing - ing.
eve - time song, ye sing - ers.

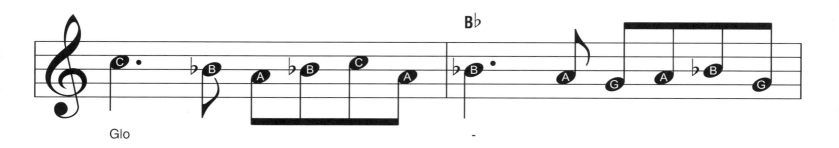

Glo -

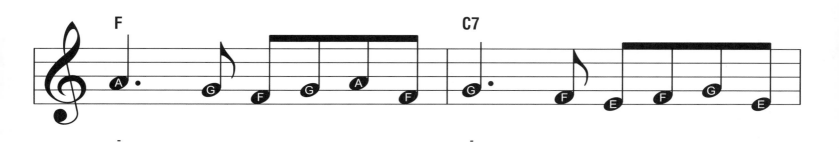

- -

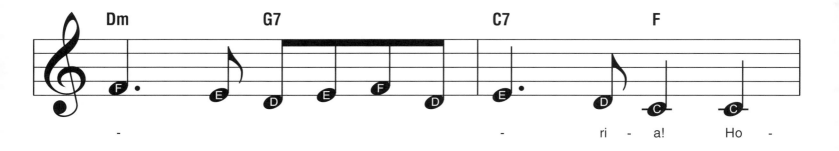

- - ri - a! Ho -

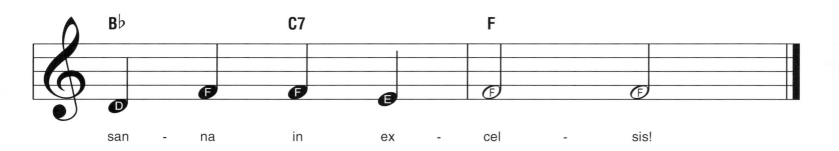

san - na in ex - cel - sis!

The First Noël

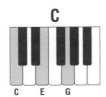
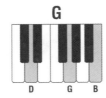
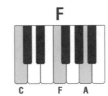
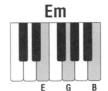

17th Century English Carol
Music from W. Sandys' *Christmas Carols*

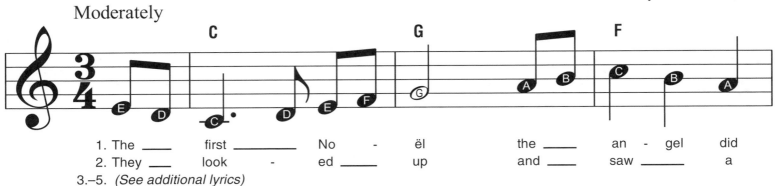

1. The ___ first _____ No - ël the ___ an - gel did
2. They ___ look - ed ___ up and ___ saw _____ a

3.–5. *(See additional lyrics)*

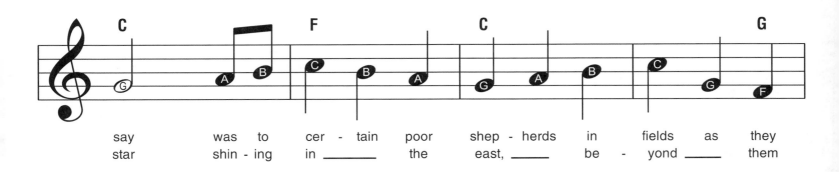

say was to cer - tain poor shep - herds in fields as they
star shin - ing in _____ the east, _____ be - yond _____ them

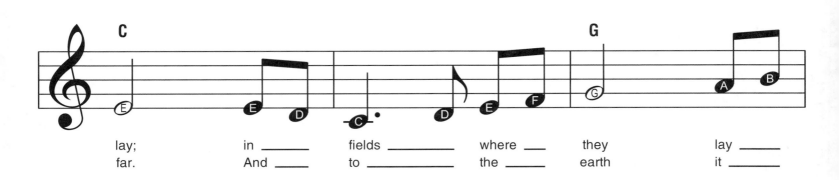

lay; in _____ fields _____ where ___ they lay
far. And _____ to _____ the ___ earth it

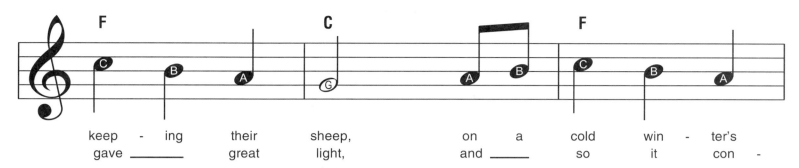

keep - ing their sheep, on a cold win - ter's
gave _____ great light, and _____ so it con -

Refrain

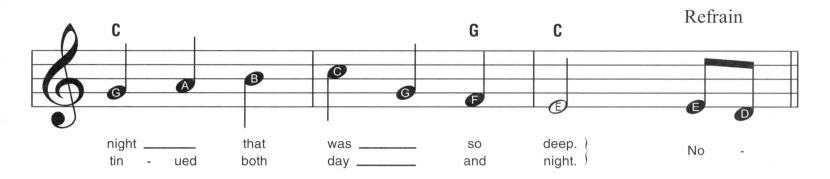

night _____ that was _____ so deep. }
tin - ued both day _____ and night. }   No -

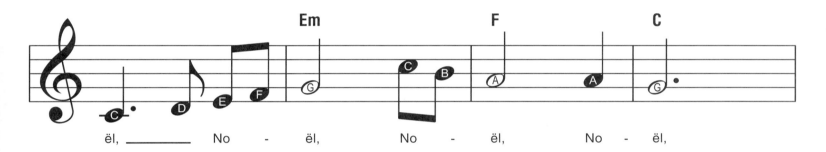

ël, _____ No - ël, No - ël, No - ël,

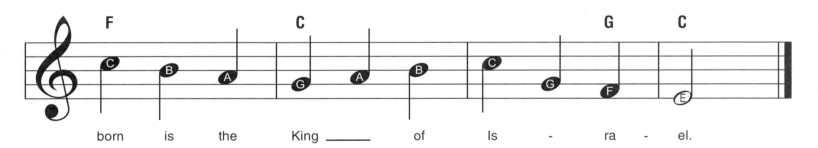

born is the King _____ of Is - ra - el.

Additional Lyrics

3. And by the light of that same star,
   Three wise men came from country far;
   To seek for a King was their intent,
   And to follow the star wherever it went.
   Refrain

4. This star drew nigh to the northwest,
   O'er Bethlehem it took its rest;
   And there it did both stop and stay,
   Right over the place where Jesus lay.
   Refrain

5. Then entered in those wise men three,
   Full reverently upon their knee;
   And offered there in His presence,
   Their gold and myrrh and frankincense.
   Refrain

Fum, Fum, Fum

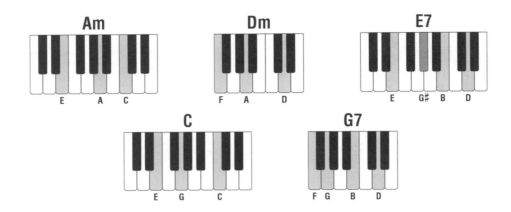

Traditional Catalonian Carol

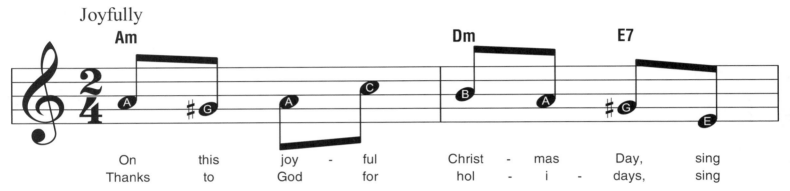

On this joy - ful Christ - mas Day, sing
Thanks to God for hol - i - days, sing

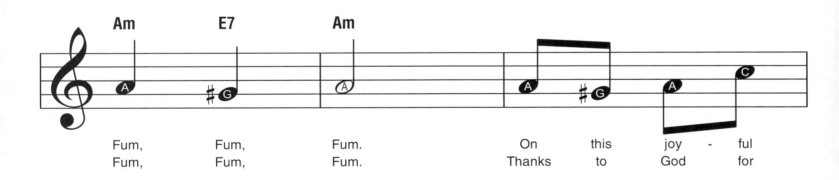

Fum, Fum, Fum. On this joy - ful
Fum, Fum, Fum. Thanks to God for

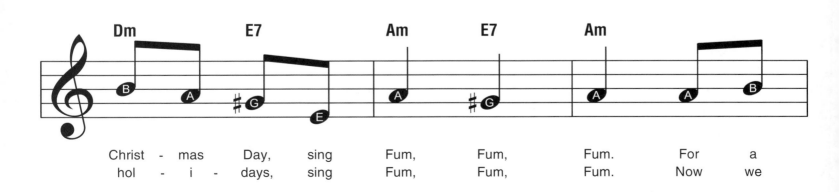

Christ - mas Day, sing Fum, Fum, Fum. For a
hol - i - days, sing Fum, Fum, Fum. Now we

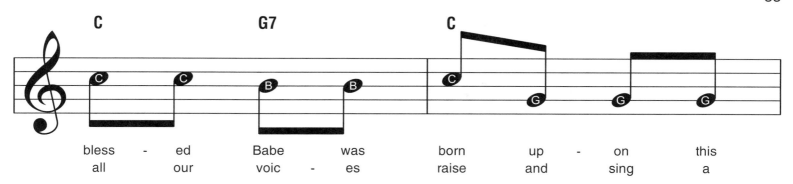

bless - ed   Babe   was   born   up - on   this
all   our   Babe   voic - es   raise   up   and   sing   a

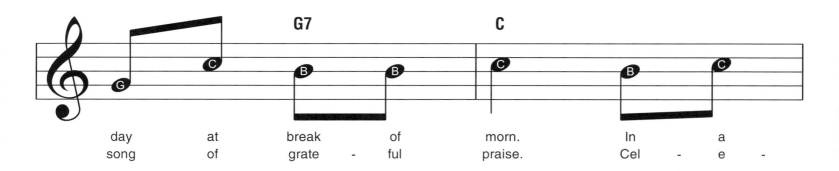

day   at   break   of   morn.   In   a
song   of   grate - ful   praise.   Cel - e -

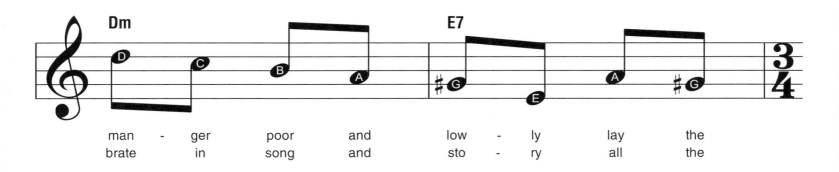

man - ger   poor   and   low - ly   lay   the
brate   in   song   and   sto - ry   all   the

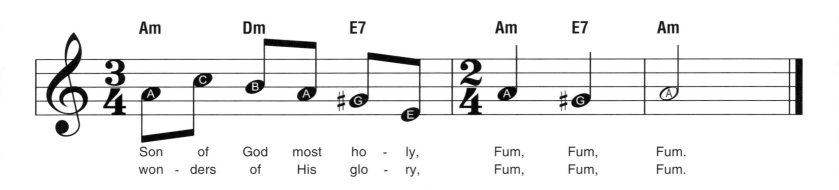

Son   of   God   most   ho - ly,   Fum,   Fum,   Fum.
won - ders   of   His   glo - ry,   Fum,   Fum,   Fum.

Go, Tell It on the Mountain

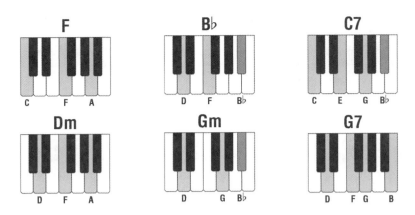

African-American Spiritual
Verses by John W. Work, Jr.

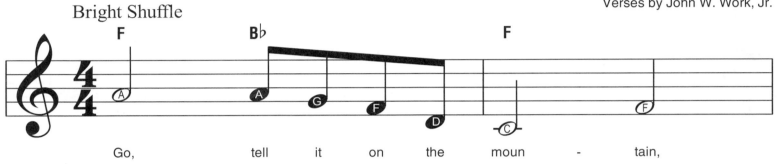

Go, tell it on the moun - tain,

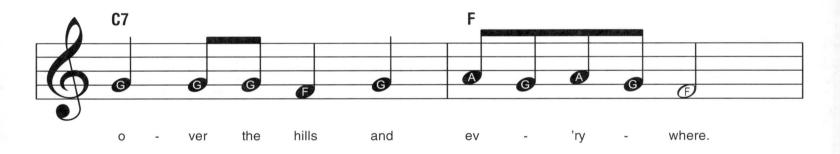

o - ver the hills and ev - 'ry - where.

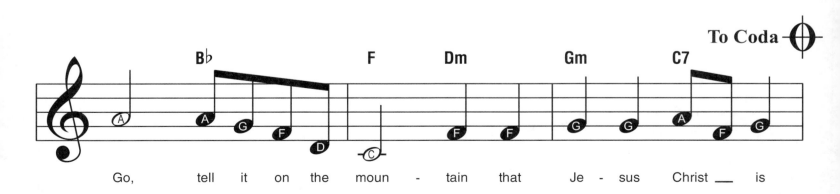

Go, tell it on the moun - tain that Je - sus Christ ___ is

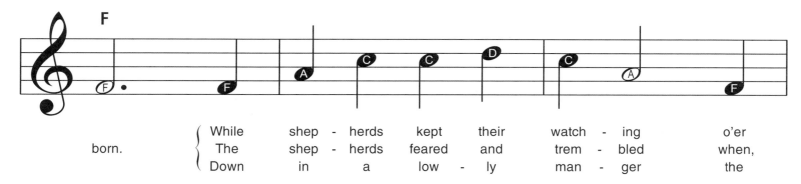

born. While shep - herds kept their watch - ing o'er
The shep - herds feared and trem - bled when,
Down in a low - ly man - ger when the

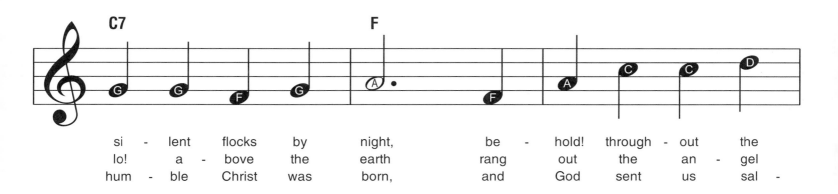

si - lent flocks by night, be - hold! through - out the
lo! a - bove the earth rang out the an - gel
hum - ble Christ was born, and God sent us sal -

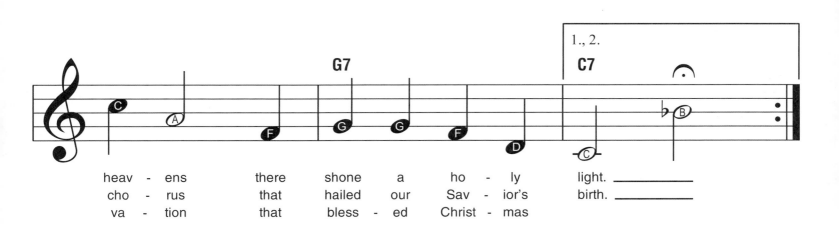

heav - ens there shone a ho - ly light. _____
cho - rus that hailed our Sav - ior's birth. _____
va - tion that bless - ed Christ - mas

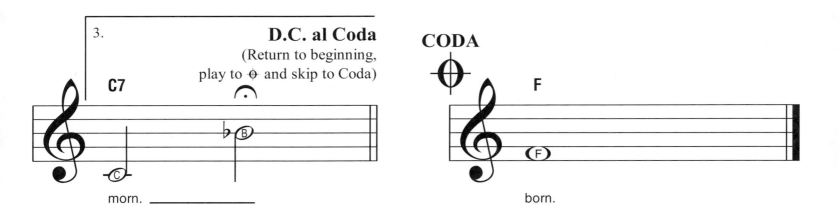

morn. _____   born.

God Rest Ye Merry, Gentlemen

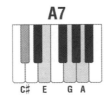
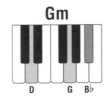
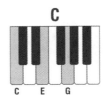
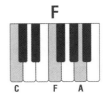

Traditional English Carol

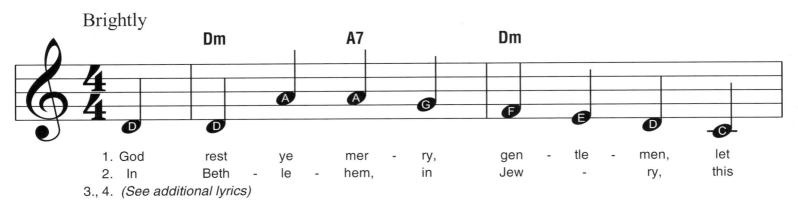

1. God rest ye mer - ry, gen - tle - men, let
2. In Beth - le - hem, in Jew - ry, this
3., 4. *(See additional lyrics)*

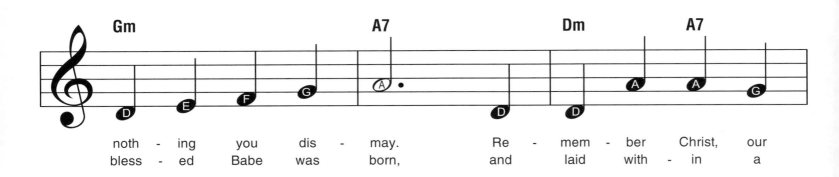

noth - ing you dis - may. Re - mem - ber Christ, our
bless - ed Babe was born, and laid with - in a

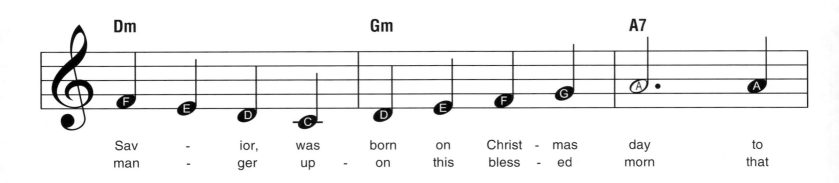

Sav - ior, was born on Christ - mas day to
man - ger up - on this bless - ed morn that

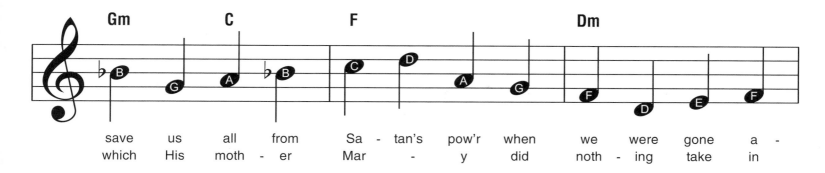

save us all from Sa - tan's pow'r when we were gone a -
which His moth - er Mar - y did noth - ing take in

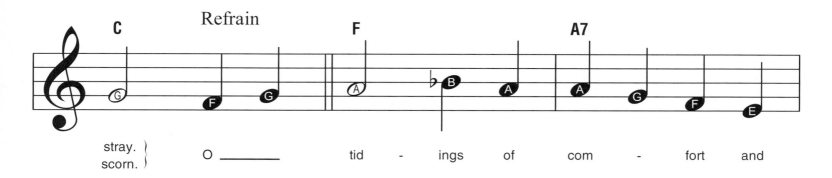

Refrain

stray. }
scorn. } O _____ tid - ings of com - fort and

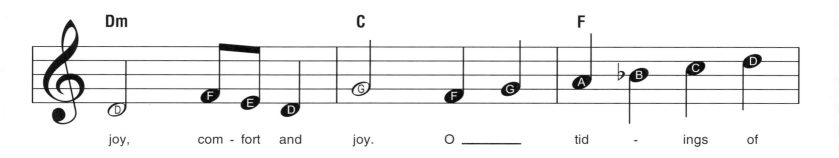

joy, com - fort and joy. O _____ tid - ings of

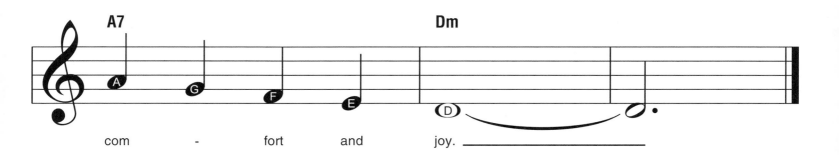

com - fort and joy. _____

Additional Lyrics

3. From God, our heav'nly Father, a blessed angel came,
   And unto certain shepherds brought tidings of the same;
   How that in Bethlehem was born the Son of God by name.
   Refrain

4. Now shepherds at those tidings rejoiced much in mind,
   And left their flocks afeeding in tempest, storm and wind,
   And went to Bethlehem straightway, the Son of God to find.
   Refrain

Good Christian Men, Rejoice

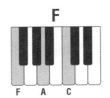
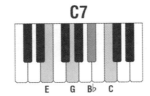

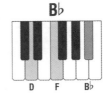

14th Century Latin Text
Translated by John Mason Neale
14th Century German Melody

Brightly

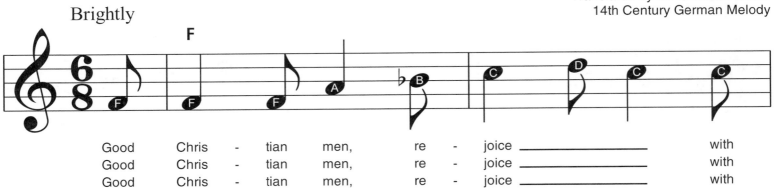

Good Chris - tian men, re - joice _____ with
Good Chris - tian men, re - joice _____ with
Good Chris - tian men, _____ with

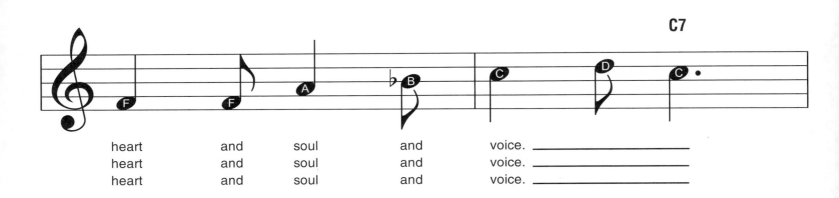

heart and soul and voice. _____
heart and soul and voice. _____
heart and soul and voice. _____

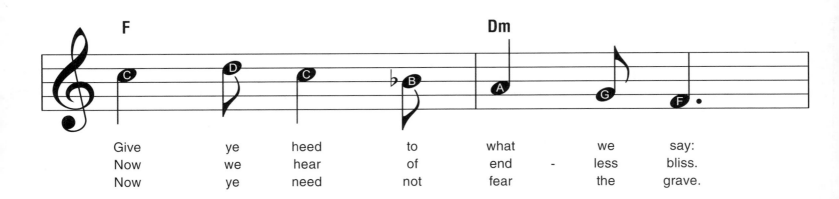

Give ye heed to what we say:
Now we hear of end - less bliss.
Now ye need not fear the grave.

Good King Wenceslas

 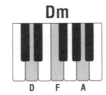 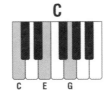 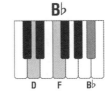

Words by John M. Neale
Music from *Piae Cantiones*

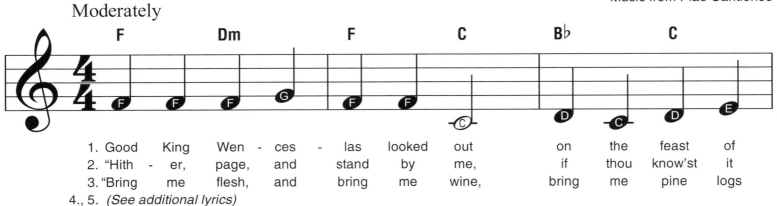

1. Good King Wen - ces - las looked out on the feast of
2. "Hith - er, page, and stand by me, if thou know'st it
3. "Bring me flesh, and bring me wine, bring me pine logs

4., 5. *(See additional lyrics)*

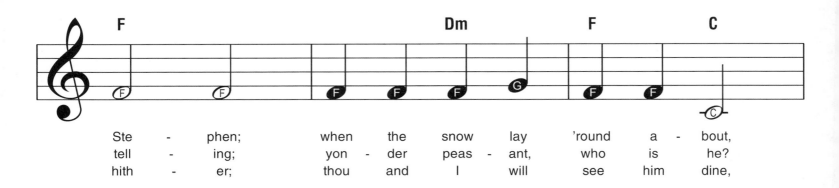

Ste - phen; when the snow lay 'round a - bout,
tell - ing; yon - der peas - ant, who is he?
hith - er; thou and I will see him dine,

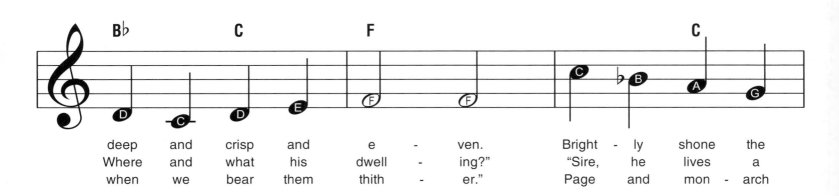

deep and crisp and e - ven. Bright - ly shone the
Where and and what his dwell - ing?" "Sire, he lives a
when we bear them thith - er." Page and mon - arch

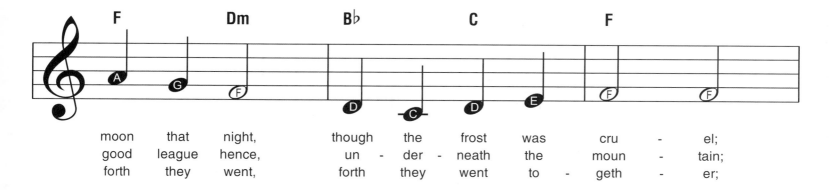

moon	that	night,	though	the	frost	was	cru	-	el;
good	league	hence,	un -	der -	neath	the	moun	-	tain;
forth	they	went,	forth	they	went	to -	geth	-	er;

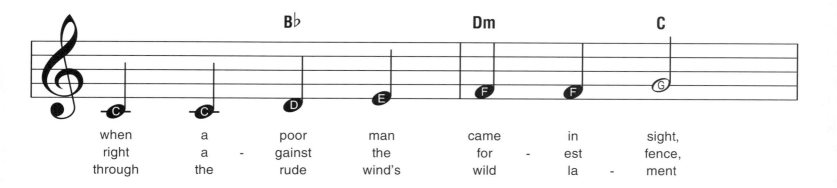

when	a	poor	man	came	in	sight,
right	a -	gainst	the	for -	est	fence,
through	the	rude	wind's	wild	la -	ment

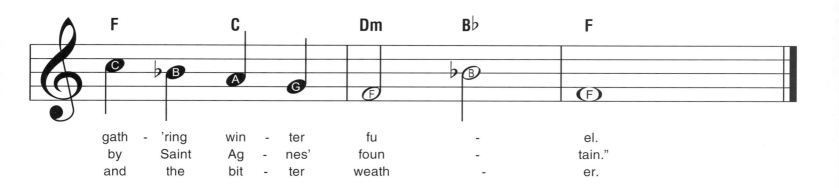

gath -	'ring	win -	ter	fu	-	el.
by	Saint	Ag -	nes'	foun	-	tain."
and	the	bit -	ter	weath	-	er.

Additional Lyrics

4. "Sire, the night is darker now,
   And the wind blows stronger;
   Fails my heart, I know not how,
   I can go no longer."
   "Mark my footsteps, my good page,
   Tread thou in them boldly;
   Thou shalt find the winter's rage
   Freeze thy blood less coldly."

5. In his master's steps he trod,
   Where the snow lay dinted;
   Heat was in the very sod
   Which the saint has printed.
   Therefore, Christian men, be sure,
   Wealth or rank possessing;
   Ye who now will bless the poor
   Shall yourselves find blessing.

Hark! The Herald Angels Sing

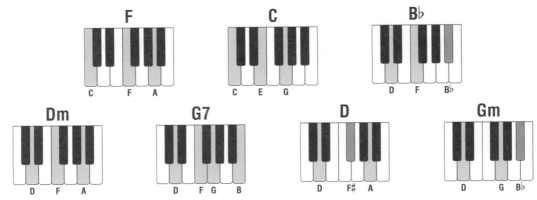

Words by Charles Wesley
Altered by George Whitefield
Music by Felix Mendelssohn-Bartholdy
Arranged by William H. Cummings

Moderately

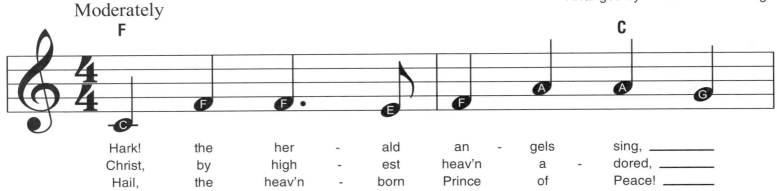

Hark! the her - ald an - gels sing, _____
Christ, by high - est heav'n a - dored, _____
Hail, the heav'n - born Prince of Peace! _____

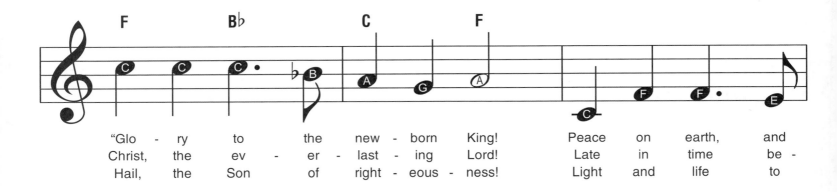

"Glo - ry to the new - born King! Peace on earth, and
Christ, the ev - er - last - ing Lord! Late in time be - to
Hail, the Son of right - eous - ness! Light and life to

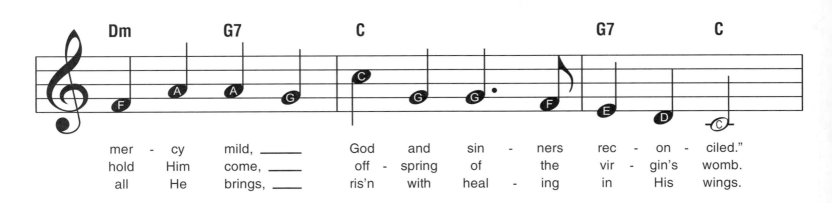

mer - cy mild, _____ God and sin - ners rec - on - ciled."
hold Him come, _____ off - spring of the vir - gin's womb.
all He brings, _____ ris'n with heal - ing in His wings.

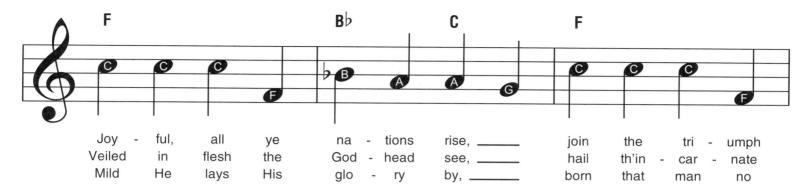

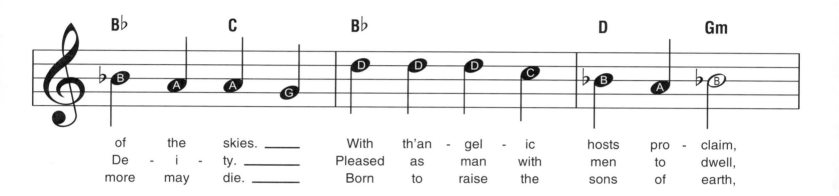

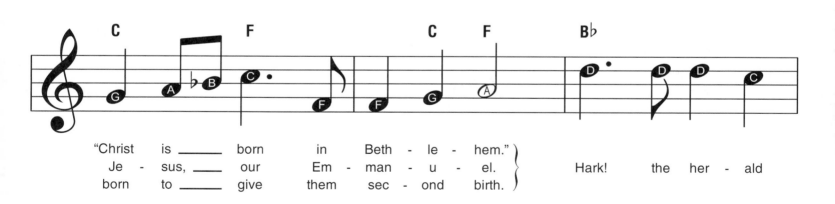

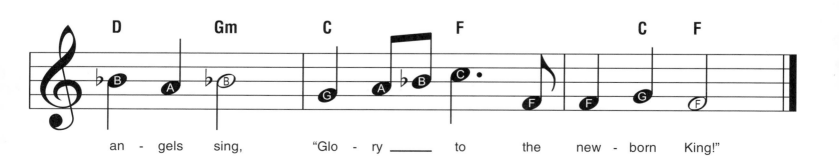

He Is Born, the Holy Child
(Il est ne, le divin enfant)

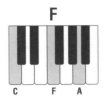 F
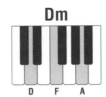 Dm
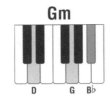 Gm
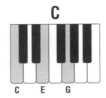 C
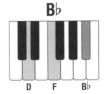 Bb

Traditional French Carol

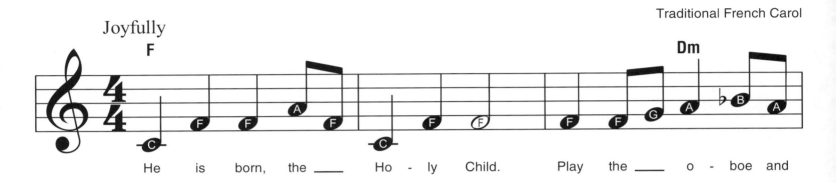

He is born, the ___ Ho - ly Child. Play the ___ o - boe and

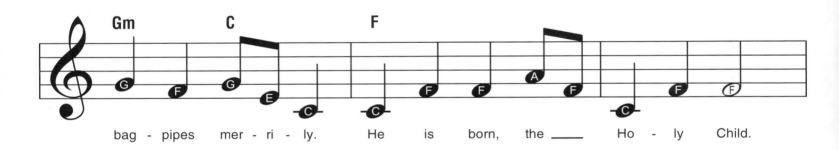

bag - pipes mer - ri - ly. He is born, the ___ Ho - ly Child.

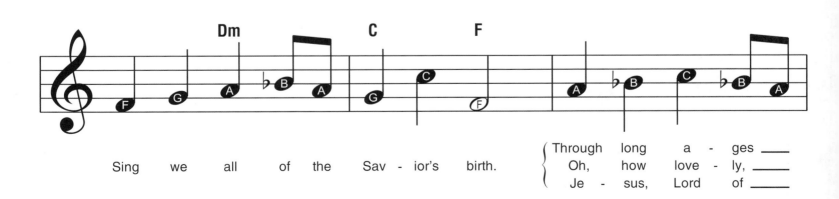

Sing we all of the Sav - ior's birth.
{ Through long a - ges ___
{ Oh, how love - ly, ___
{ Je - sus, Lord of ___

45

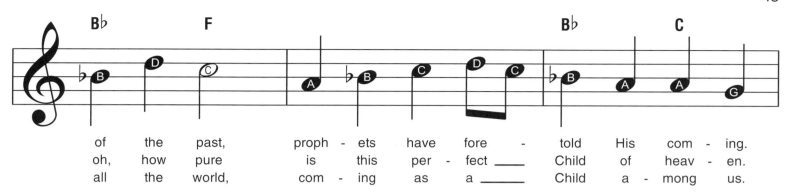

of the past, proph - ets have fore - told His com - ing.
oh, how pure is this per - fect ___ Child of heav - en.
all the world, com - ing as a ___ Child a - mong us.

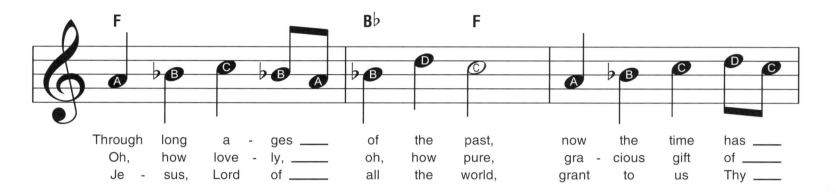

Through long a - ges ___ of the past, now the time has ___
Oh, how love - ly, ___ oh, how pure, gra - cious gift of ___
Je - sus, Lord of ___ all the world, grant to us Thy ___

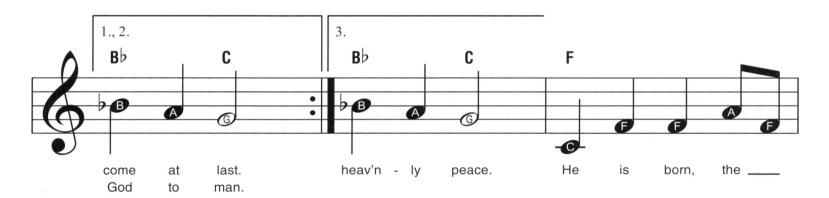

1., 2.
come at last.
God to man.

3.
heav'n - ly peace. He is born, the ___

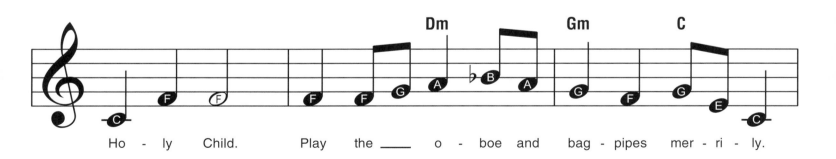

Ho - ly Child. Play the ___ o - boe and bag - pipes mer - ri - ly.

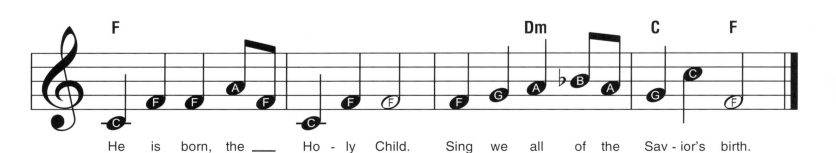

He is born, the ___ Ho - ly Child. Sing we all of the Sav - ior's birth.

Here We Come A-Wassailing

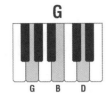 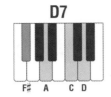 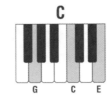 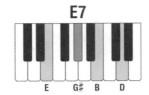 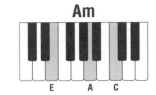

Traditional

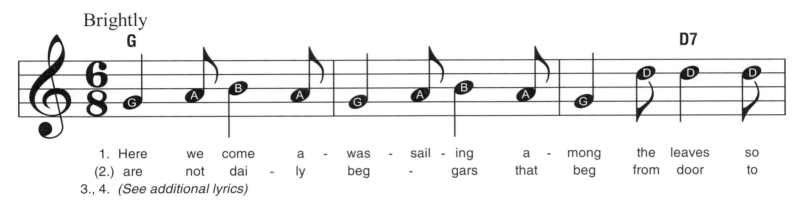

1. Here we come a - was - sail - ing a - mong the leaves so
(2.) are not dai - ly beg - gars that beg from door to

3., 4. *(See additional lyrics)*

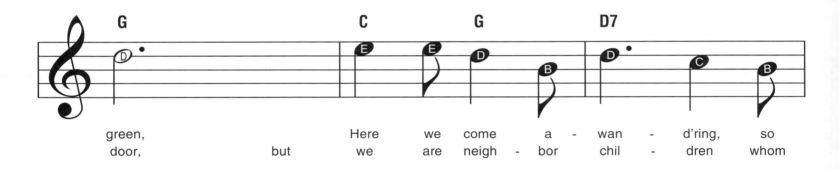

green,   Here we come a - wan - d'ring, so
door,   but   we   are   neigh - bor chil - dren   whom

Refrain

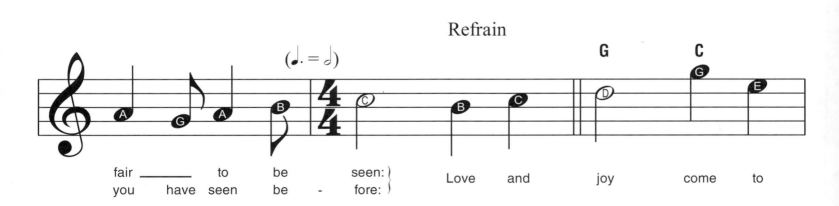

fair _____ to be seen: Love and joy come to
you have seen be - fore:

47

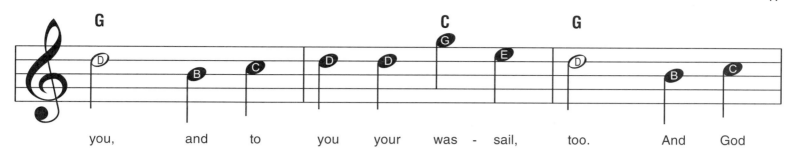

you, and to you your was - sail, too. And God

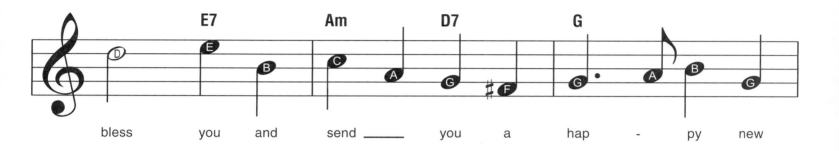

bless you and send _____ you a hap - py new

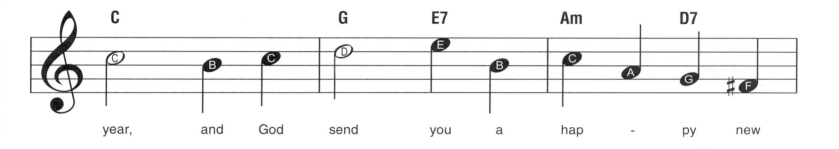

year, and God send you a hap - py new

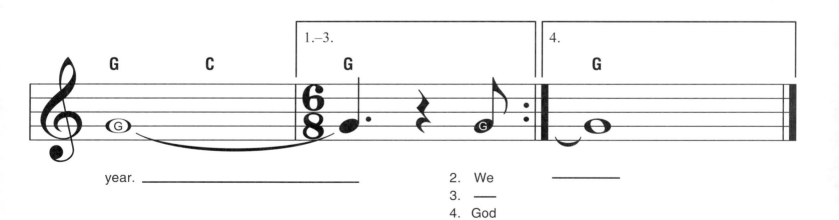

year. _____ 2. We _____
                                3. —
                                4. God

Additional Lyrics

3. We have got a little purse
   Of stretching leather skin;
   We want a little money
   To line the well within.
   Refrain

4. God bless the master of this house,
   Likewise the mistress, too;
   And all the little children
   That round the table go.
   Refrain

The Holly and the Ivy

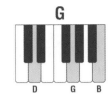
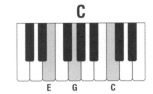
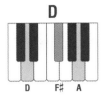

18th Century English Carol

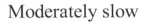

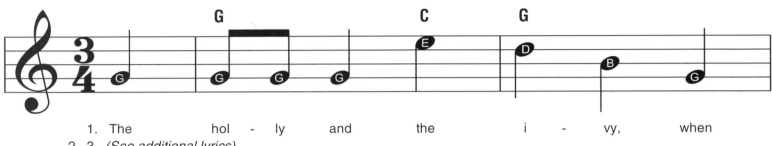

1. The hol-ly and the i-vy, when
2., 3. *(See additional lyrics)*

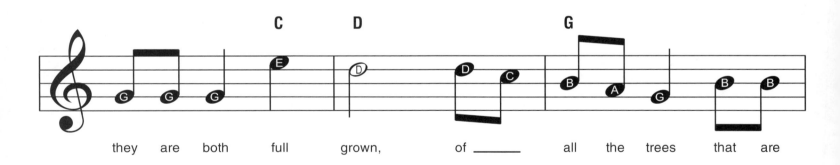

they are both full grown, of _____ all the trees that are

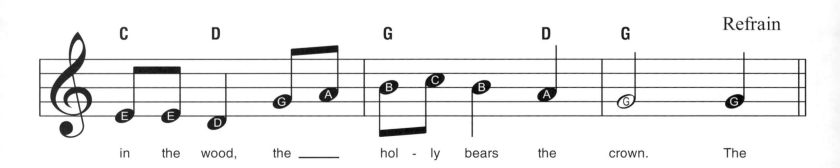

in the wood, the _____ hol-ly bears the crown. The

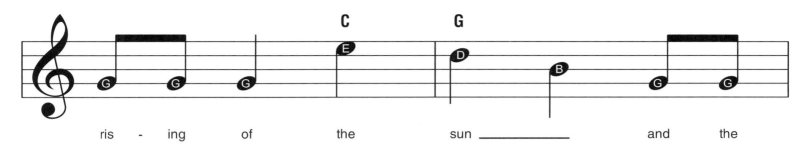

ris - ing of the sun _____ and the

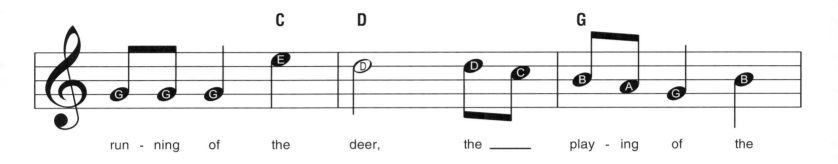

run - ning of the deer, the _____ play - ing of the

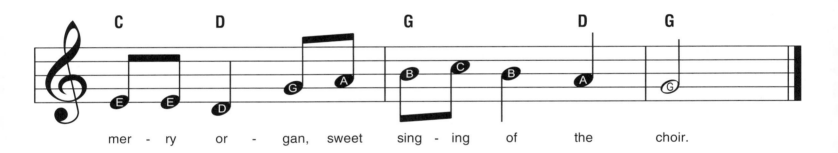

mer - ry or - gan, sweet sing - ing of the choir.

Additional Lyrics

2. The holly bears a blossom
   As white as lily flow'r,
   And Mary bore sweet Jesus Christ
   To be our sweet Savior.
   Refrain

3. The holly bears a berry
   As red as any blood,
   And Mary bore sweet Jesus Christ
   To do poor sinners good.
   Refrain

The Huron Carol
('Twas in the Moon of Wintertime)

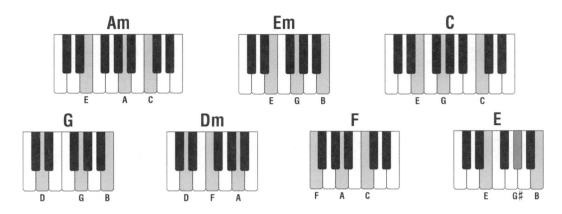

Traditional French-Canadian Text
Traditional Canadian-Indian Melody

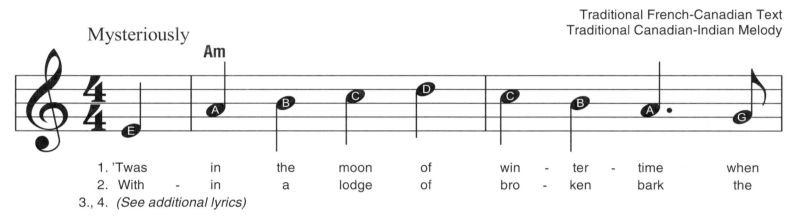

1. 'Twas   in   the   moon   of   win - ter - time   when
2. With - in   a   lodge   of   bro - ken   bark   when   the

3., 4. *(See additional lyrics)*

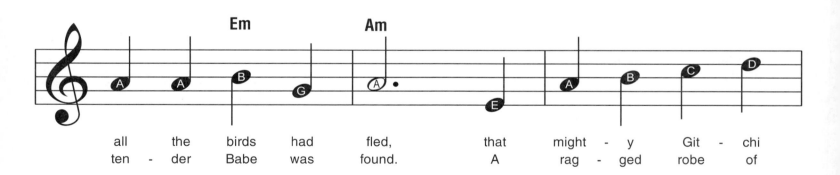

all   the   birds   had   fled,   that   might - y   Git - chi
ten - der   Babe   was   found.   A   rag - ged   robe   of

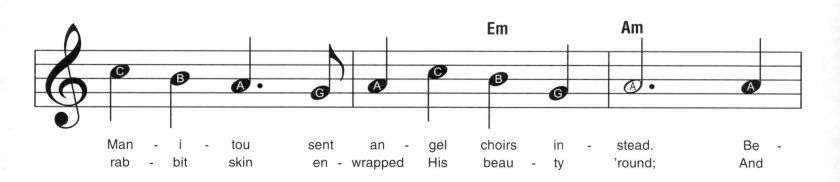

Man - i - tou   sent   an - gel   choirs   in - stead.   Be -
rab - bit   skin   en - wrapped   His   beau - ty   'round;   And

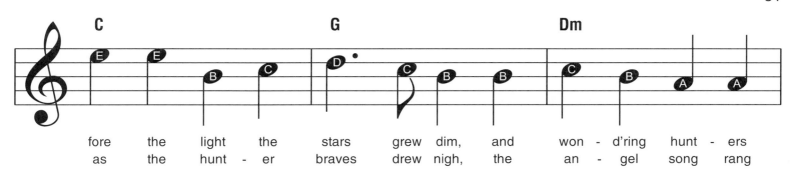

fore the light the stars grew dim, and the won - d'ring hunt - ers
as the hunt - er braves drew nigh, and the an - gel song rang

Refrain

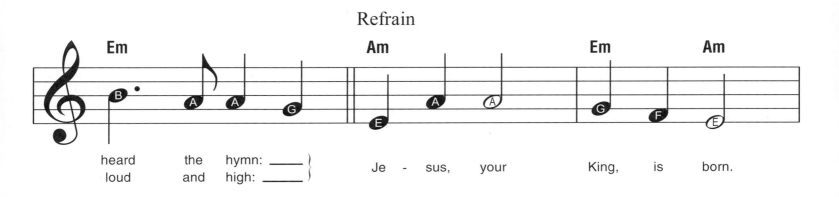

heard the hymn: _____ } Je - sus, your King, is born.
loud and high: _____ }

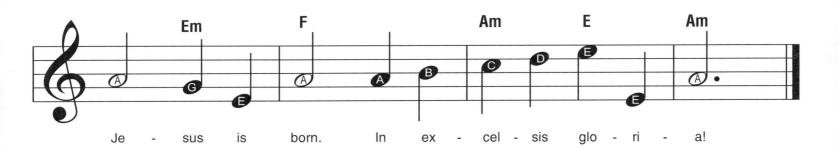

Je - sus is born. In ex - cel - sis glo - ri - a!

Additional Lyrics

3. The earliest moon of wintertime is not so round and fair
   As was the ring of glory or the helpless Infant there.
   The chiefs from far before Him knelt with gifts of fur and beaver pelt.
   Refrain

4. O children of the forest free, O sons of Manitou,
   The Holy Child of earth and heav'n is born today for you.
   Come kneel before the radiant Boy who brings you beauty, peace and joy.
   Refrain

I Heard the Bells on Christmas Day

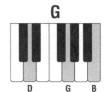 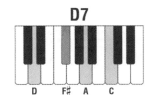 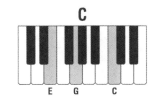 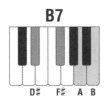 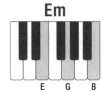

Words by Henry Wadsworth Longfellow
Music by John Baptiste Calkin

Moderately

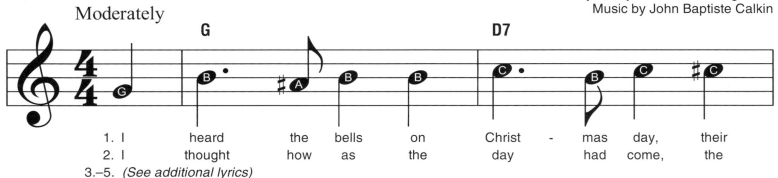

1. I heard the bells on Christ - mas day, their
2. I thought how as on the day had come, the

3.–5. *(See additional lyrics)*

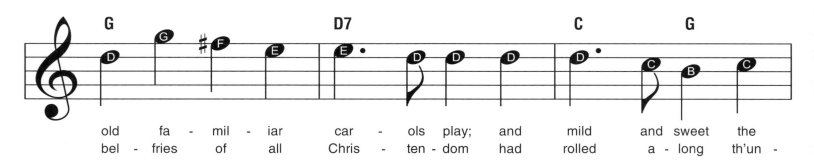

old fa - mil - iar car - ols play; and mild and sweet the
bel - fries of all Chris - ten - dom had rolled a - long th'un -

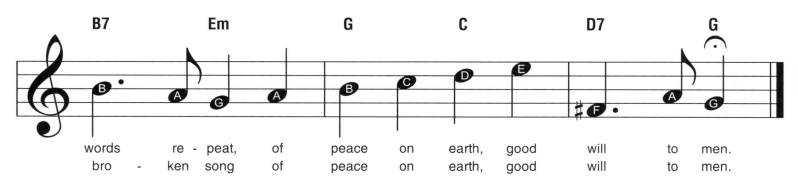

words re - peat, of peace on earth, good will to men.
bro - ken song of peace on earth, good will to men.

Additional Lyrics

3. And in despair I bowed my head:
"There is no peace on earth," I said,
"For hate is strong, and mocks the song
Of peace on earth, good will to men."

4. Then pealed the bells more loud and deep:
"God is not dead, nor doth He sleep;
The wrong shall fail, the right prevail,
With peace on earth, good will to men."

5. Till ringing, singing on its way,
The world revolved from night to day;
A voice, a chime, a chant sublime,
Of peace on earth, good will to men!

I Saw Three Ships

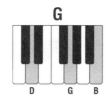 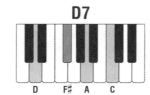 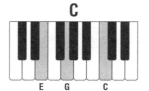

Traditional English Carol

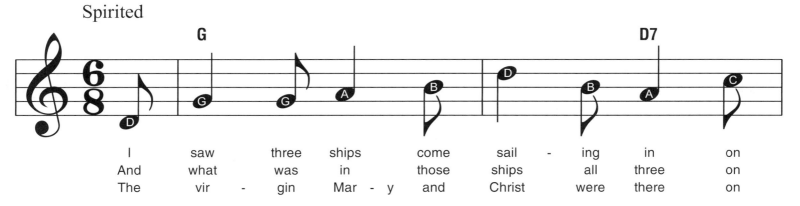

I saw three ships come sail - ing in on
And saw what was in those ships all in three on
The vir - gin Mar - y and Christ were there on

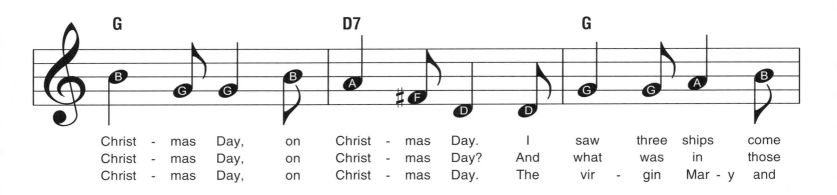

Christ - mas Day, on Christ - mas Day. I saw three ships come
Christ - mas Day, on Christ - mas Day? And saw what was in those
Christ - mas Day, on Christ - mas Day. The vir - gin Mar - y and

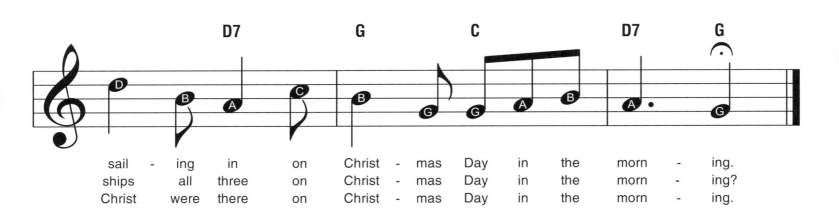

sail - ing in on Christ - mas Day in the morn - ing.
ships all three on Christ - mas Day in the morn - ing?
Christ were there on Christ - mas Day in the morn - ing.

In the Bleak Midwinter

 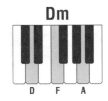 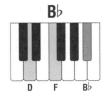 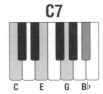

Poem by Christina Rossetti
Music by Gustav Holst

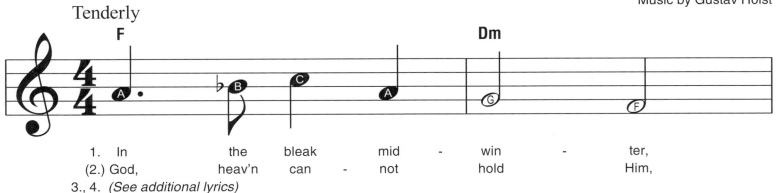

1. In the bleak mid - win - ter,
(2.) God, heav'n can - not hold Him,
3., 4. *(See additional lyrics)*

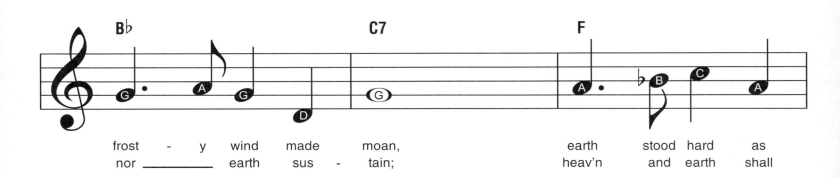

frost - y wind made moan, earth stood hard as
nor _____ earth made sus - tain; heav'n and earth shall

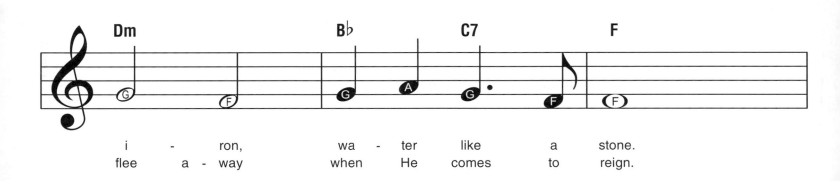

i - ron, wa - ter like a stone.
flee a - way when He comes to reign.

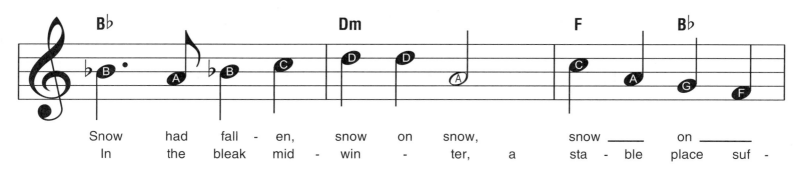

Snow had fall - en, snow on snow, snow _____ on _____
In the bleak mid - win - ter, a sta - ble place suf -

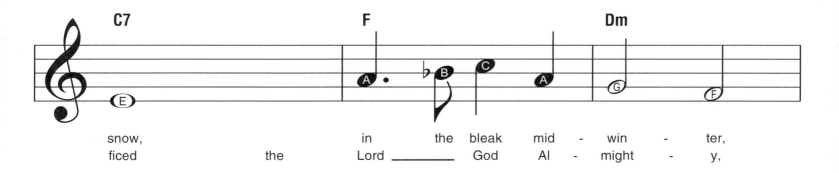

snow, in the bleak mid - win - ter,
ficed the Lord _____ God Al - might - y,

long _____ a - go. 2. Our heart.
Je - sus Christ.

Additional Lyrics

3. Angels and archangels may have gathered there,
   Cherubim and seraphim thronged the air.
   But His mother only, in her maiden bliss,
   Worshiped the Beloved with a kiss.

4. What can I give Him, poor as I am?
   If I were a shepherd, I would bring a lamb.
   If I were a wise man, I would do my part.
   Yet, what can I give Him? Give my heart.

It Came Upon the Midnight Clear

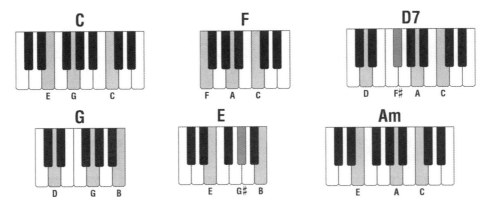

Words by Edmund Hamilton Sears
Music by Richard Storrs Willis

Moderately

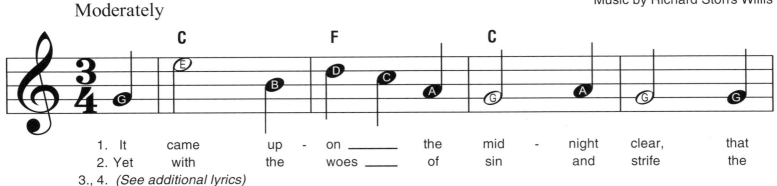

1. It came up - on _____ the mid - night clear, that
2. Yet with the woes _____ of sin and strife that the

3., 4. *(See additional lyrics)*

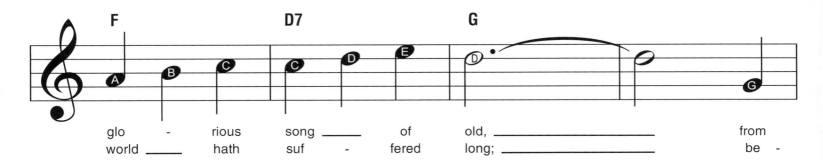

glo - rious song _____ of old, _____ from
world _____ hath suf - fered long; _____ be -

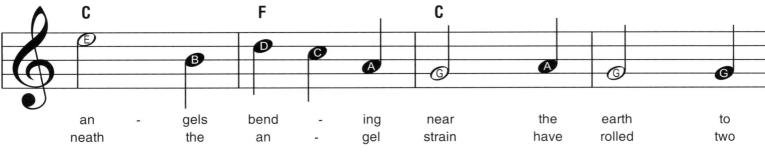

an - gels bend - ing near the earth to
neath the an - gel strain have earth rolled two

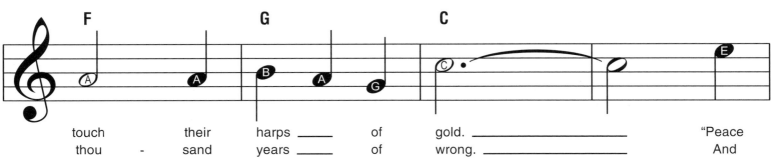

touch their harps _____ of gold. _____ "Peace
thou - sand years _____ of wrong. _____ And

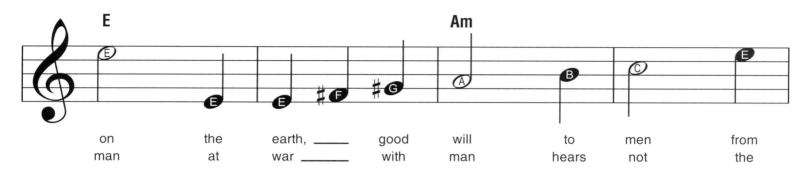

on the earth, _____ good will to men from
man at war _____ with man hears not the

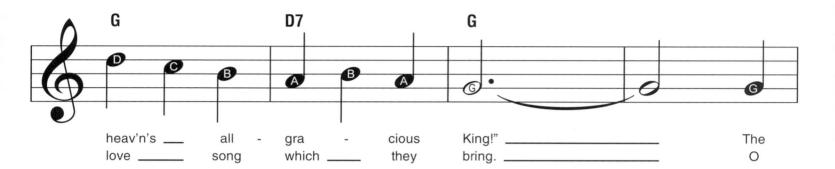

heav'n's ___ all - gra - cious King!" _____ The
love _____ song which _____ they bring. _____ O

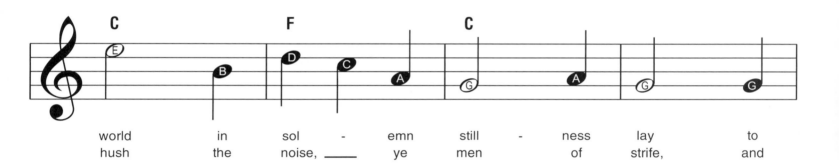

world in sol - emn still - ness lay to
hush the noise, _____ ye men of strife, and

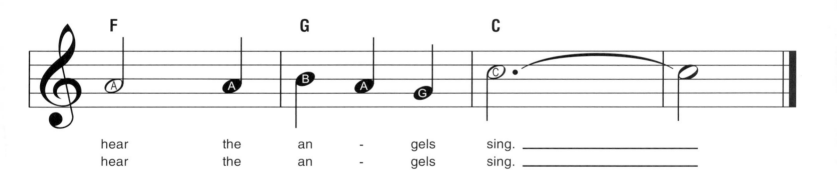

hear the an - gels sing. _____
hear the an - gels sing. _____

Additional Lyrics

3. And ye, beneath life's crushing load,
 Whose forms are bending low,
 Who toil along the climbing way
 With painful steps and slow;
 Look now, for glad and golden hours
 Come swiftly on the wing.
 O rest beside the weary road
 And hear the angels sing.

4. For lo, the days are hast'ning on,
 By prophet bards foretold,
 When with the ever-circling years
 Comes round the age of gold;
 When peace shall over all the earth
 Its ancient splendors fling,
 And the whole world give back the song
 Which now the angels sing.

Jingle Bells

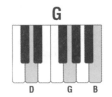
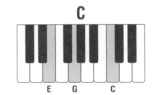
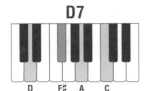
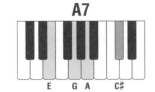

Words and Music by
J. Pierpont

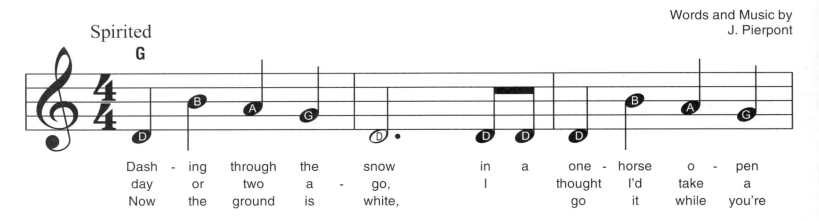

Dash	-	ing	through	the	snow		in	a	one	-	horse	o	-	pen
day	or	two	a	-	go,		I		thought	I'd	take	a		
Now	the	two	ground	is	white,				go	it	take	while	you're	

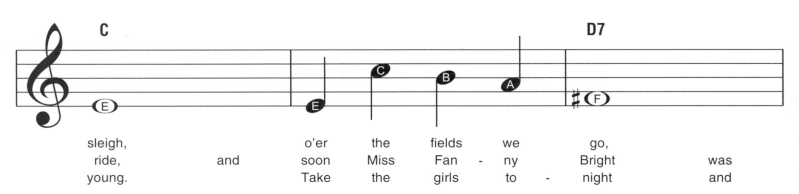

sleigh,			o'er	the	fields	we		go,		
ride,	and		soon	Miss	Fan	-	ny	Bright	was	
young.		Take	the	girls	to	-	night	and		

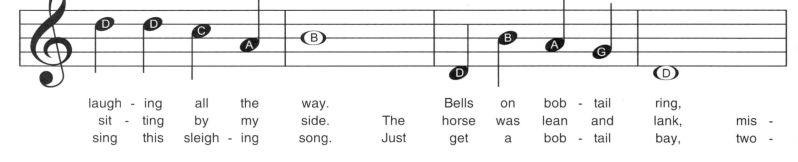

laugh	-	ing	all	the	way.	Bells	on	bob	-	tail	ring,	
sit	-	ting	by	my	side.	The	horse	was	lean	and	lank,	mis -
sing	this	sleigh	-	ing	song.	Just	get	a	bob	-	tail	bay,	two -

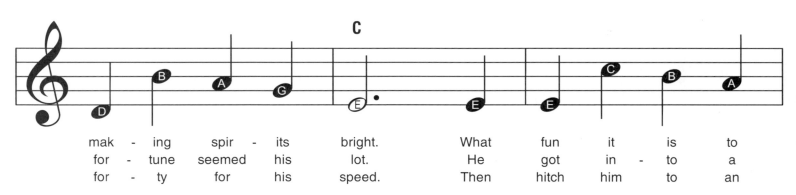

mak	-	ing	spir	-	its	bright.	What	fun	it	is	to
for	-	tune	seemed	his	lot.	He	got	in	-	to	a
for	-	ty	for	his	speed.	Then	hitch	him	to	an	

Jolly Old St. Nicholas

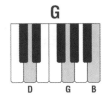 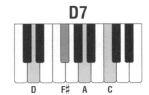 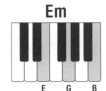 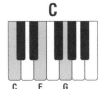

Traditional 19th Century American Carol

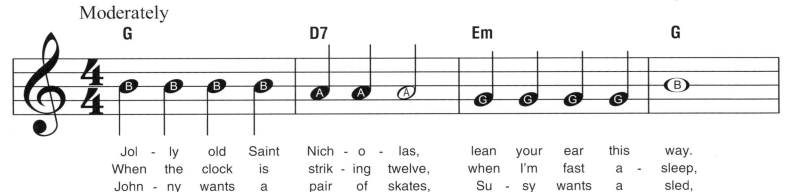

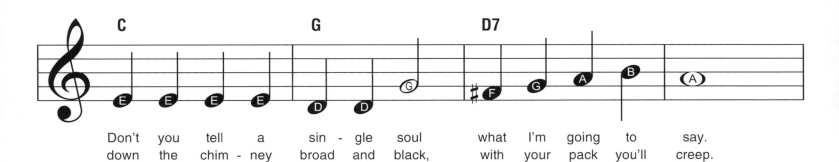

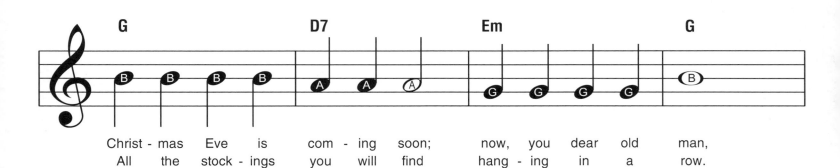

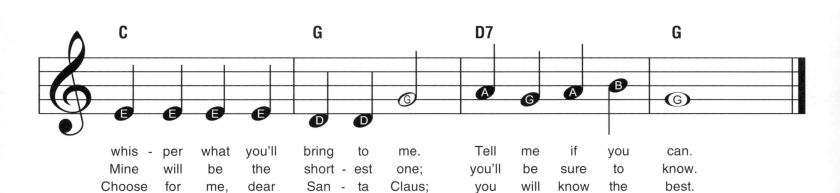

Mary Had a Baby

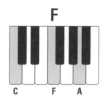 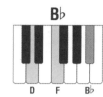 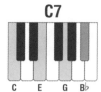 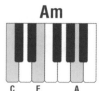 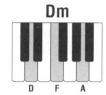

African-American Spiritual

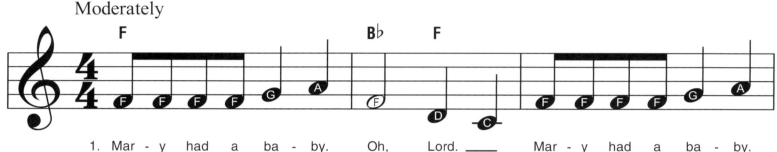

1. Mar - y had a ba - by. Oh, Lord. _____ Mar - y had a ba - by.
2. What _____ did she name Him? Oh, Lord. _____ What _____ did she name Him?
3. She _____ called Him Je - sus. Oh, Lord. _____ She _____ called Him Je - sus.

4.–7. *(See additional lyrics)*

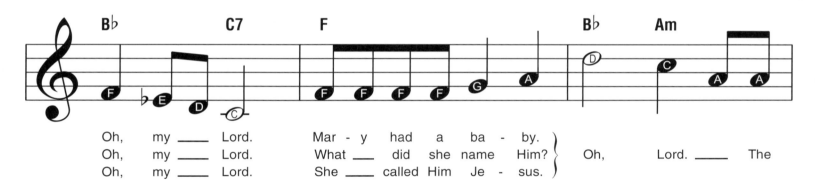

Oh, my _____ Lord. Mar - y had a ba - by.
Oh, my _____ Lord. What _____ did she name Him? } Oh, Lord. _____ The
Oh, my _____ Lord. She _____ called Him Je - sus.

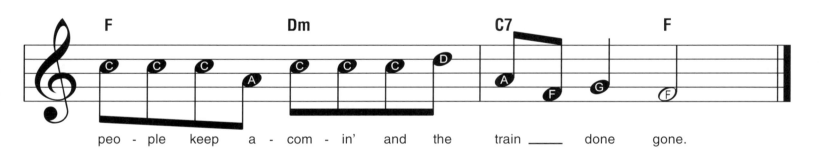

peo - ple keep a - com - in' and the train _____ done gone.

Additional Lyrics

4. Where was He born? Oh, Lord...

5. Born in a stable. Oh, Lord...

6. Where did they lay Him? Oh, Lord...

7. Laid Him in a manger. Oh, Lord...

Joy to the World

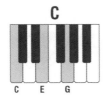
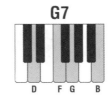
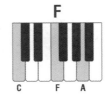

Words by Isaac Watts
Music by George Frideric Handel
Adapted by Lowell Mason

Joyfully

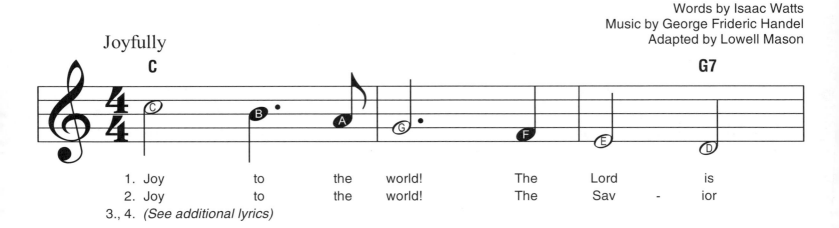

1. Joy to the world! The Lord is
2. Joy to the world! The Sav - ior
3., 4. *(See additional lyrics)*

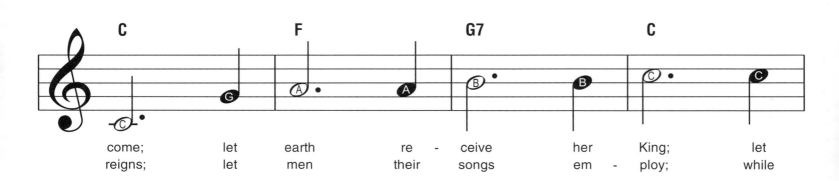

come; let earth re - ceive her King; let
reigns; let men their songs em - ploy; while

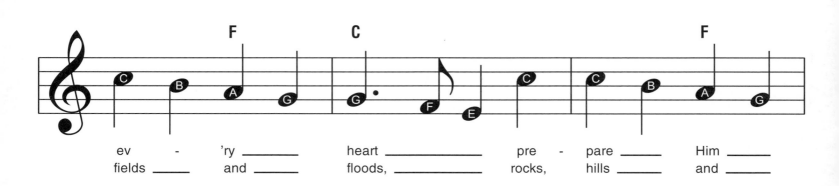

ev - 'ry _____ heart _____ pre - pare _____ Him _____
fields _____ and _____ floods, _____ rocks, hills _____ and _____

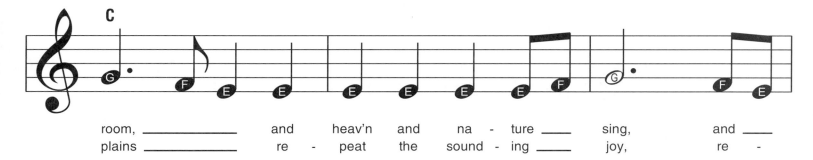

room, _____ and heav'n and na - ture ____ sing, and ____
plains _____ re - peat the sound - ing ____ joy, re -

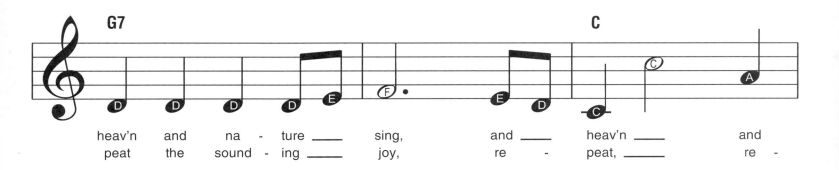

heav'n and na - ture ____ sing, and ____ heav'n ____ and
peat the sound - ing ____ joy, re - peat, _____ re -

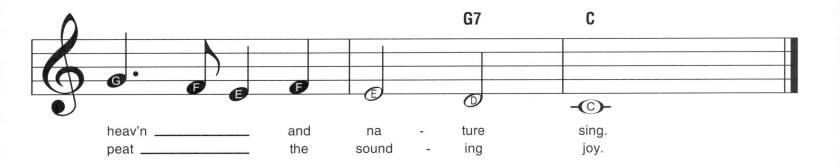

heav'n _____ and na - ture sing.
peat _____ the sound - ing joy.

Additional Lyrics

3. No more let sin and sorrow grow,
Nor thorns infest the ground.
He comes to make His blessings flow
Far as the curse is found,
Far as the curse is found,
Far as, far as the curse is found.

4. He rules the world with truth and grace,
And makes the nations prove
The glories of His righteousness,
And wonders of His love,
And wonders of His love,
And wonders, wonders of His love.

Lo, How a Rose E'er Blooming

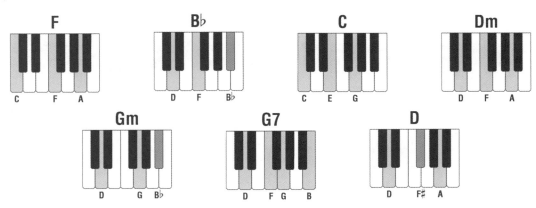

15th Century German Carol
Translated by Theodore Baker
Music from *Alte Catholische Geistliche Kirchengesang*

Tenderly

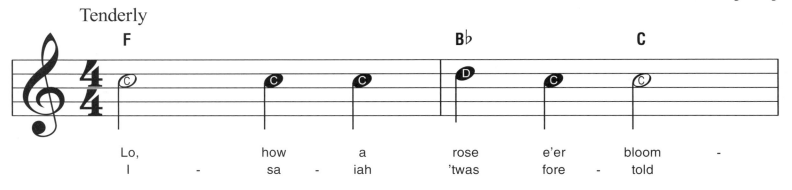

Lo,   how   a   rose   e'er   bloom -
I -   sa -   iah   'twas   fore -   told

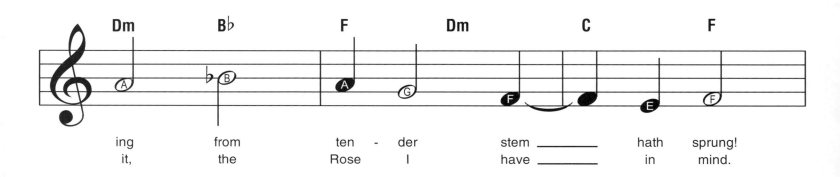

ing   from   ten - der   stem _____ hath   sprung!
it,   the   Rose   I   have _____ in   mind.

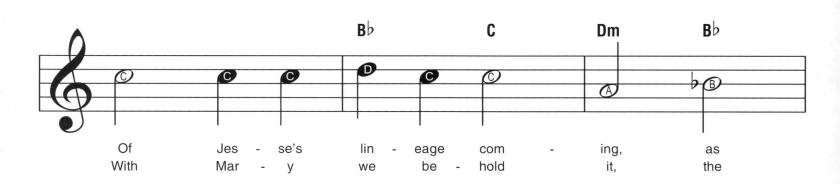

Of   Jes - se's   lin - eage com - ing,   as
With   Mar - y   we   be - hold   it,   the

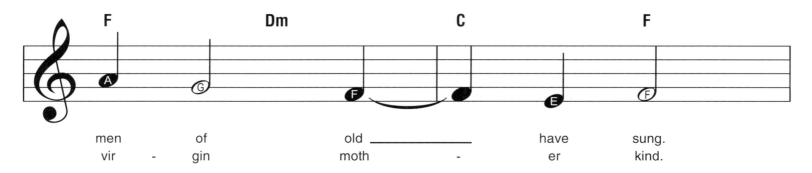

men   of   old _____ have   sung.
vir - gin   moth -   er   kind.

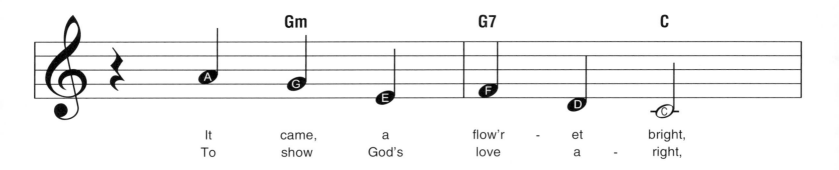

It   came,   a   flow'r - et   bright,
To   show   God's   love   a - right,

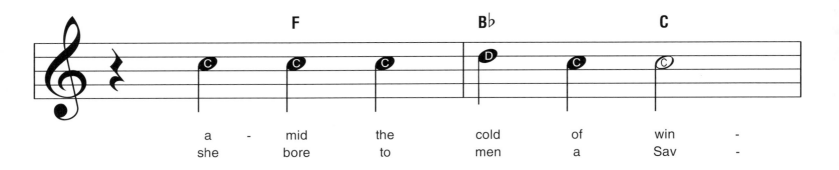

a - mid   the   cold   of   win -
she   bore   to   men   a   Sav -

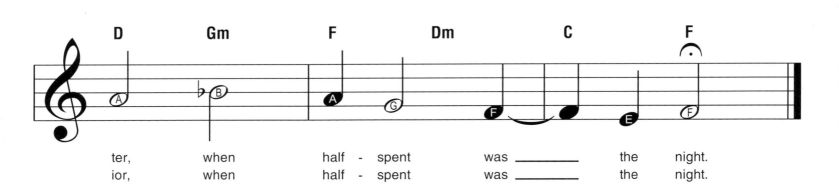

ter,   when   half - spent   was _____ the   night.
ior,   when   half - spent   was _____ the   night.

Masters in This Hall

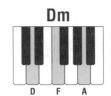 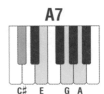 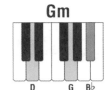 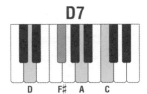 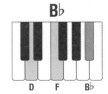

Traditional English

1. Mas - ters in this hall, _____ hear ye news to -
2. Then to Beth - 'lem town _____ we went two and
3. There - in did we see _____ sweet and good - ly

4., 5. *(See additional lyrics)*

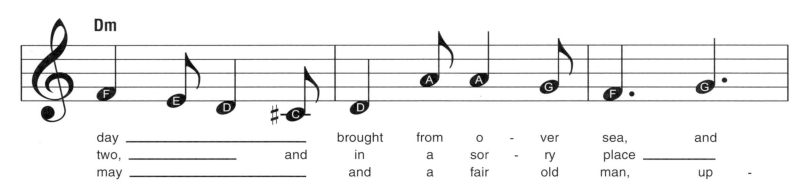

day _____ brought from o - ver sea, and
two, _____ and in a sor - ry place _____
may _____ and a fair old man, up -

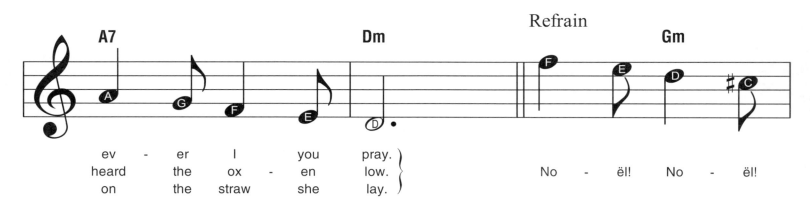

ev - er I you pray. }
heard the ox - en low. } No - ël! No - ël!
on the straw she lay. }

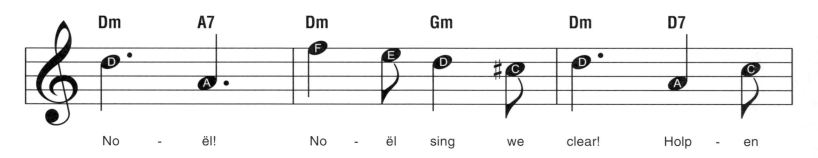

No - ël! No - ël sing we clear! Holp - en

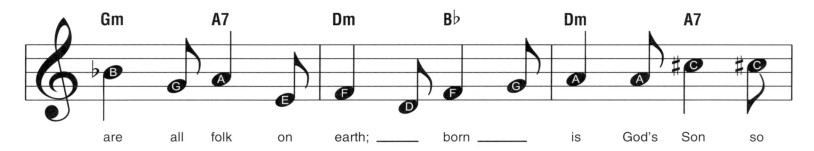

are all folk on earth; _____ born _____ is God's Son so

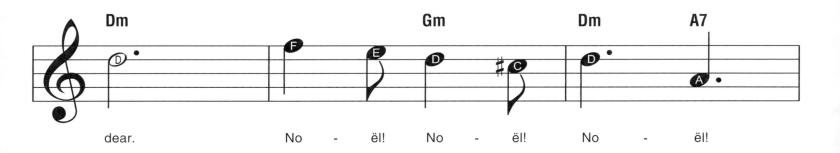

dear. No - ël! No - ël! No - ël!

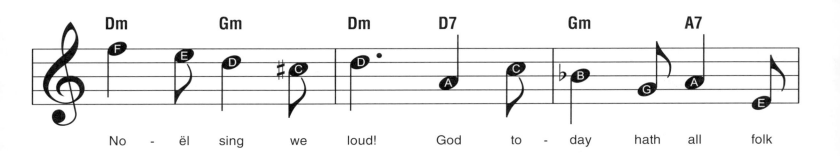

No - ël sing we loud! God to - day hath all folk

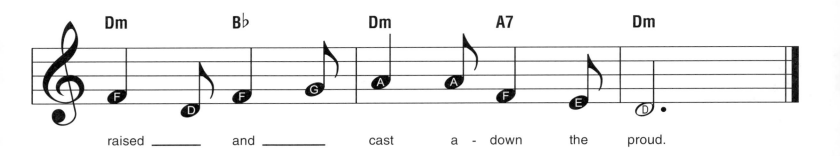

raised _____ and _____ cast a - down the proud.

Additional Lyrics

4. And a little Child
   On her arm had she.
   "Wot ye who this is?"
   Said the hinds to me.
   Refrain

5. This is Christ the Lord;
   Masters, be ye glad.
   Christmas is come in
   And no folk should be sad.
   Refrain

O Christmas Tree

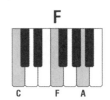
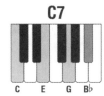
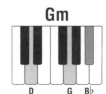
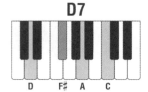

Traditional German Carol

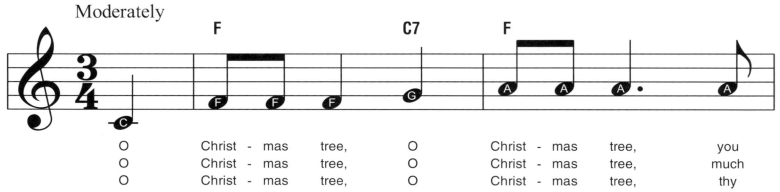

O Christ - mas tree, O Christ - mas tree, you
O Christ - mas tree, O Christ - mas tree, much
O Christ - mas tree, O Christ - mas tree, thy

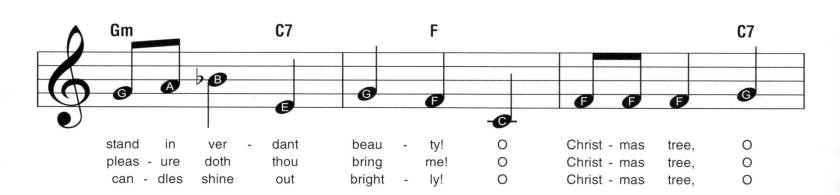

stand in ver - dant beau - ty! O Christ - mas tree, O
pleas - ure doth thou bring me! O Christ - mas tree, O
can - dles shine out bright - ly! O Christ - mas tree, O

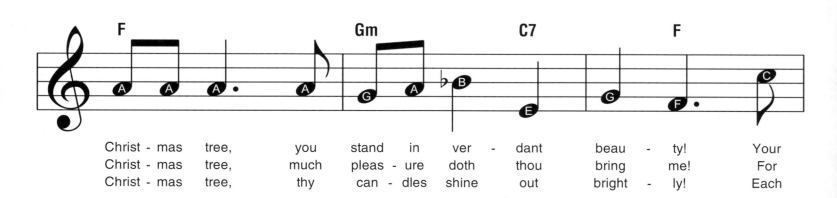

Christ - mas tree, you stand in ver - dant beau - ty! Your
Christ - mas tree, much pleas - ure doth thou bring me! For
Christ - mas tree, thy can - dles shine out bright - ly! Each

69

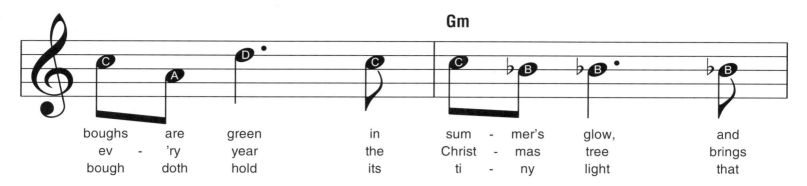

boughs are green in sum - mer's glow, and
ev - 'ry year in the Christ - mas tree brings
bough doth hold its ti - ny light that

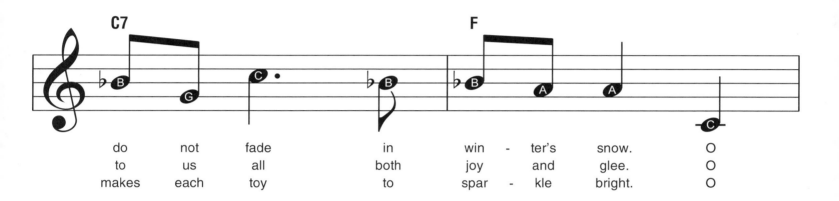

do not fade in win - ter's snow. O
to us all both joy and glee. O
makes each toy to spar - kle bright. O

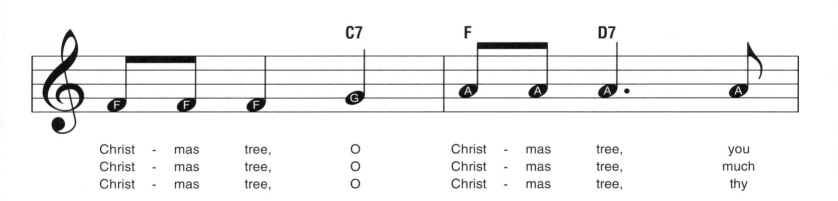

Christ - mas tree, O Christ - mas tree, you
Christ - mas tree, O Christ - mas tree, much
Christ - mas tree, O Christ - mas tree, thy

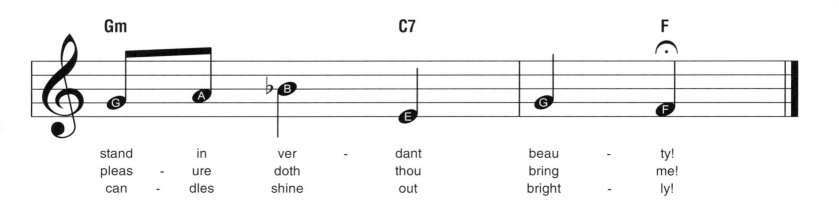

stand in ver - dant beau - ty!
pleas - ure doth thou bring me!
can - dles shine out bright - ly!

O Come, All Ye Faithful

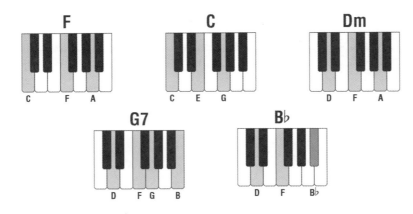

Music by John Francis Wade
Latin Words translated by Frederick Oakeley

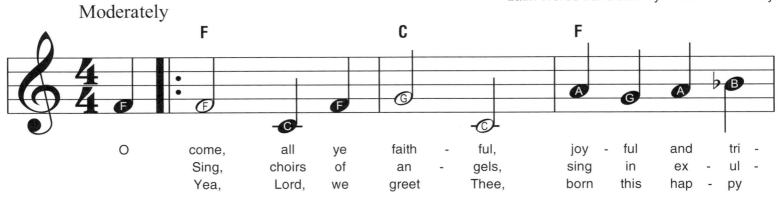

O come, all ye faith - ful, joy - ful and tri -
Sing, choirs of an - gels, sing in ex - ul -
Yea, Lord, we greet Thee, born this hap - py

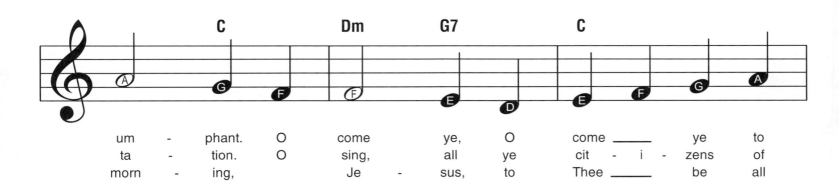

um - phant. O come ye, O come ____ ye to
ta - tion. O sing, all ye cit - i - zens of
morn - ing, Je - sus, to Thee ____ be all

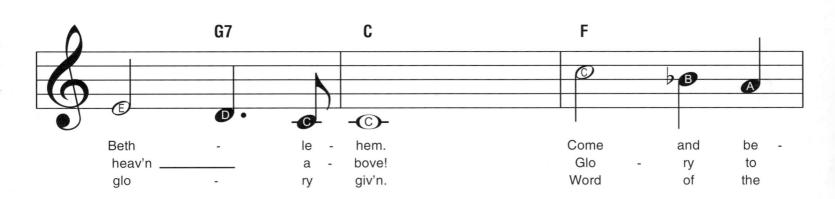

Beth - le - hem. Come and be -
heav'n ____ a - bove! Glo - ry to
glo - ry giv'n. Word of the

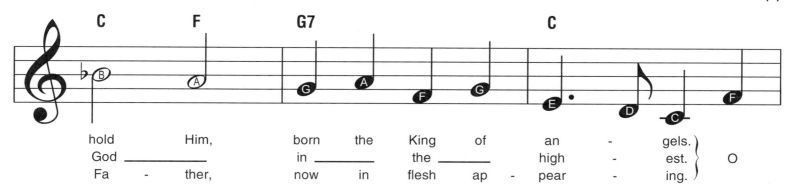

hold Him, born the King of an - gels.
God _____ in _____ the _____ high - est. } O
Fa - ther, now in flesh ap - pear - ing. }

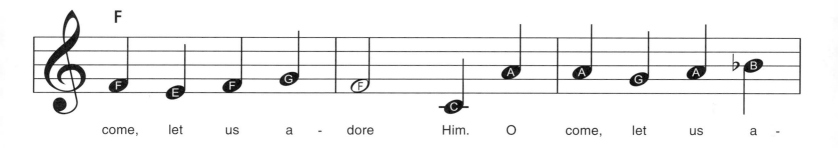

come, let us a - dore Him. O come, let us a -

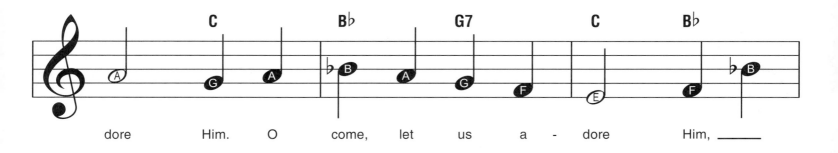

dore Him. O come, let us a - dore Him, _____

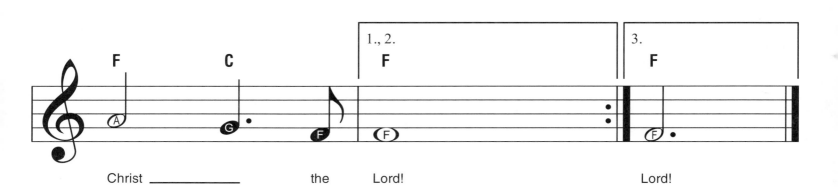

Christ _____ the Lord! | Lord!

O Come, Little Children

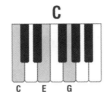 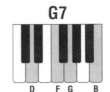 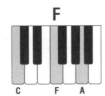

Words by C. von Schmidt
Music by J.P.A. Schulz

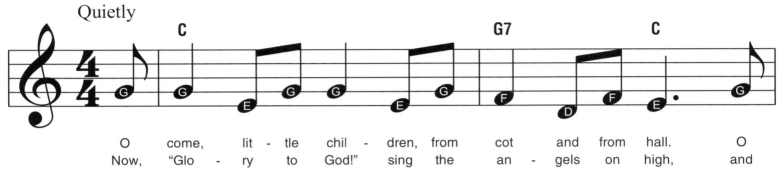

O come, lit-tle chil-dren, from cot and from hall. O
Now, "Glo-ry to God!" sing the an-gels on high, and

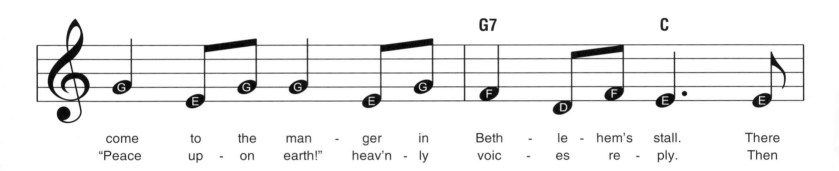

come to the man-ger in Beth-le-hem's stall. There
"Peace up-on earth!" heav'n-ly voic-es re-ply. Then

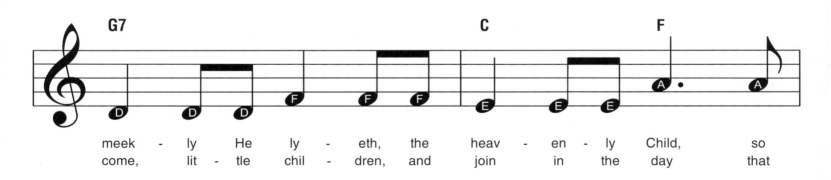

meek-ly He ly-eth, the heav-en-ly Child, so
come, lit-tle chil-dren, and join in the day that

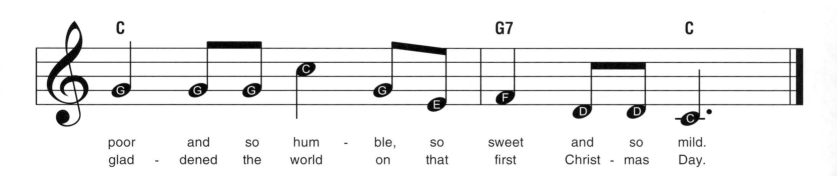

poor and so hum-ble, so sweet and so mild.
glad-ened so the world on that sweet first Christ-mas Day.

O Little Town of Bethlehem

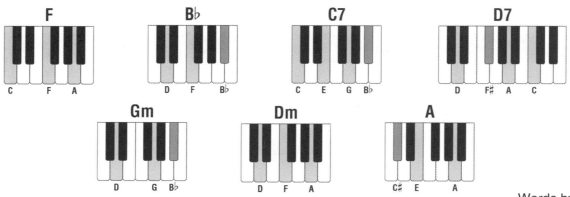

Words by Phillips Brooks
Music by Lewis H. Redner

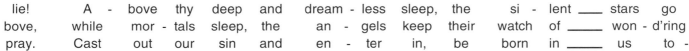

O lit- tle town of Beth- le- hem, how still we ___ see thee
For Christ is born of Mar- y, and gath- ered ___ all a-
O ho- ly Child of Beth- le- hem, de- scend to ___ us, we

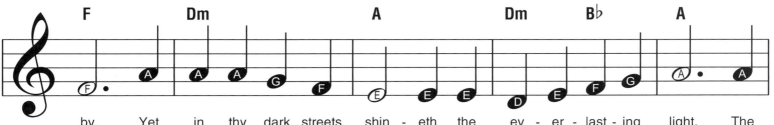

lie! A- bove thy deep and dream- less sleep, the si- lent ___ stars go
bove, while mor- tals sleep, the an- gels keep their watch of ___ won- d'ring
pray. Cast out our sin and en- ter in, be born in ___ us to-

by. Yet in thy dark streets shin- eth the ev- er- last- ing light. The
love. O morn- ing stars to- geth- er pro- claim the ho- ly birth. And
day. We hear the Christ- mas an- gels, the great glad tid- ings tell. O

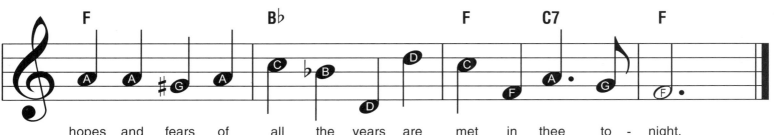

hopes and fears of all the years are met in thee to- night.
prais- es sing to God the King, and peace to men on earth.
come to us, a- bide with us, our Lord, Em- man- u- el!

O Come, O Come, Emmanuel

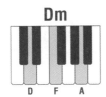
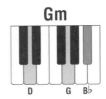
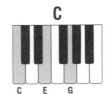
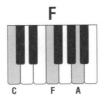
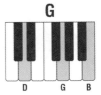

V. 1,2 translated by John M. Neale
V. 3,4 translated by Henry S. Coffin
15th Century French Melody
Adapted by Thomas Helmore

Moderately slow

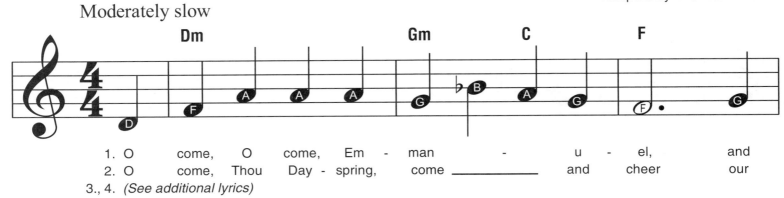

1. O come, O come, Em - man - u - el, and
2. O come, Thou Day - spring, come _____ and cheer our
3., 4. *(See additional lyrics)*

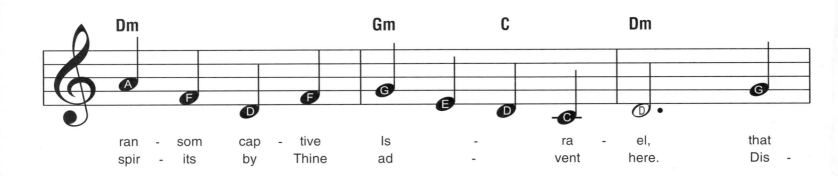

ran - som cap - tive Is - ra - el, that
spir - its by Thine ad - vent here. Dis -

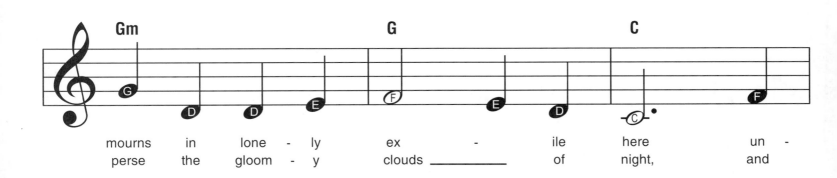

mourns in lone - ly ex - ile here un -
perse the gloom - y clouds _____ of night, and

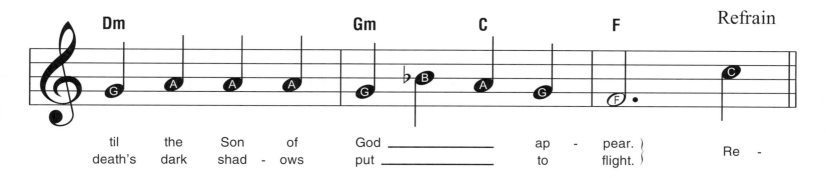

Refrain

til   the   Son   of   God _____ ap - pear.
death's dark shad - ows put _____ to flight.
Re -

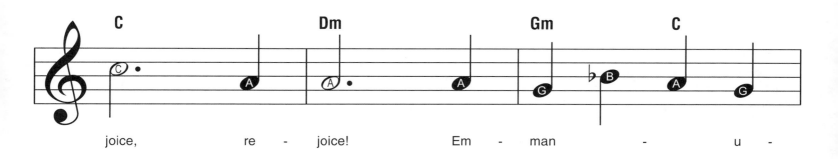

joice,   re - joice!   Em - man - u -

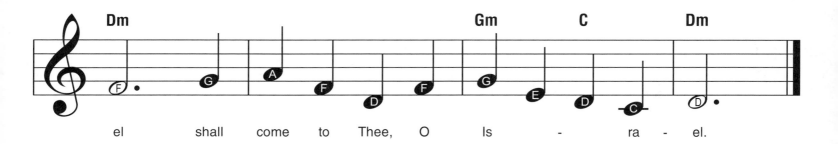

el   shall   come   to   Thee,   O   Is - ra - el.

Additional Lyrics

3. O come, Thou Wisdom from on high,
   And order all things far and nigh.
   To us the path of knowledge show,
   And cause us in her ways to go.
   Refrain

4. O come, Desire of nations, bind
   All people in one heart and mind.
   Bid envy, strife and quarrels cease;
   Fill the whole world with heaven's peace.
   Refrain

O Holy Night

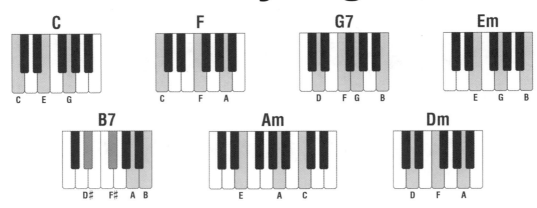

French Words by Placide Cappeau
English Words by John S. Dwight
Music by Adolphe Adam

Flowing

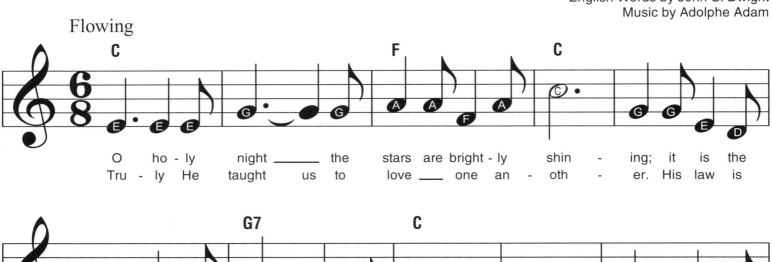

O ho-ly night ___ the stars are bright-ly shin - ing; it is the
Tru - ly He taught us to love ___ one an - oth - er. His law is

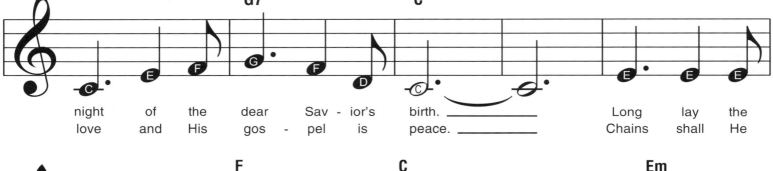

night of the dear Sav - ior's birth. ___ Long lay the
love and His gos - pel is peace. ___ Chains shall He

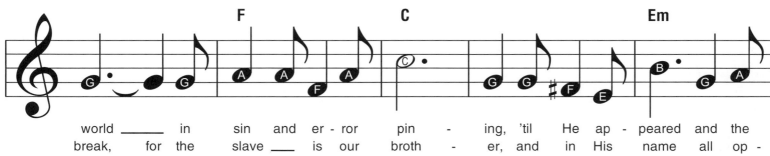

world ___ in sin and er - ror pin - ing, 'til He ap - peared and the
break, for the slave ___ is our broth - er, and in His name all op -

soul felt its worth. ___ A thrill of hope the
pres - sion shall cease. ___ Sweet hymns of joy in

Once in Royal David's City

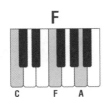
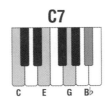
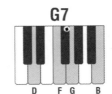
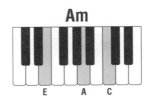
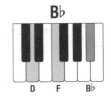

Words by Cecil F. Alexander
Music by Henry J. Gauntlett

Stately

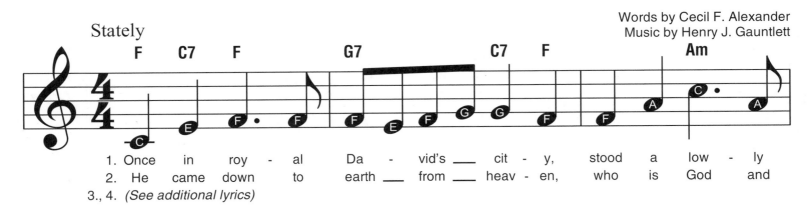

1. Once in roy - al Da - vid's city, stood a low - ly
2. He came down to earth from heav - en, who is God and
3., 4. (See additional lyrics)

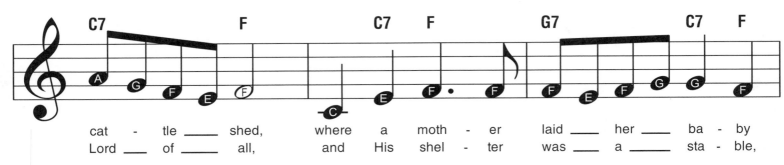

cat - tle ____ shed, where a moth - er laid ____ her ____ ba - by
Lord ____ of ____ all, and His shel - ter was ____ a ____ sta - ble,

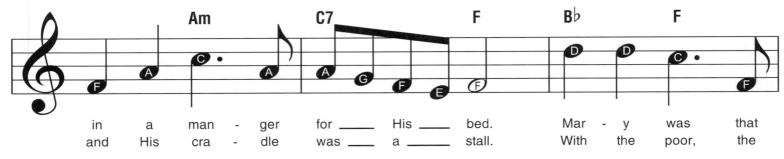

in a man - ger for ____ His ____ bed. Mar - y was that
and His cra - dle was ____ a ____ stall. With the poor, the

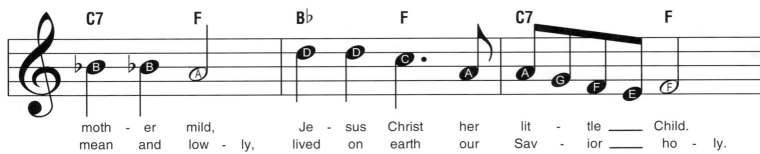

moth - er mild, Je - sus Christ her lit - tle ____ Child.
mean and low - ly, lived on earth our Sav - ior ____ ho - ly.

Additional Lyrics

3. Jesus is our childhood's pattern;
Day by day like us He grew.
He was little, weak and helpless;
Tears and smiles, like us, He knew.
And He feeleth for our sadness,
And He shareth in our gladness.

4. And our eyes at last shall see Him,
Through His own redeeming love,
For that Child so dear and gentle
Is our Lord in heav'n above.
And He leads His children on
To the place where He is gone.

Pat-a-Pan
(Willie, Take Your Little Drum)

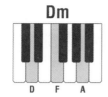
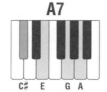
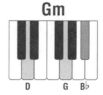

Words and Music by
Bernard de la Monnoye

Wil - lie, take your lit - tle drum. Rob - in, bring your
When the men of old - en days gave the King of
God and man to - day be - come close - ly joined as

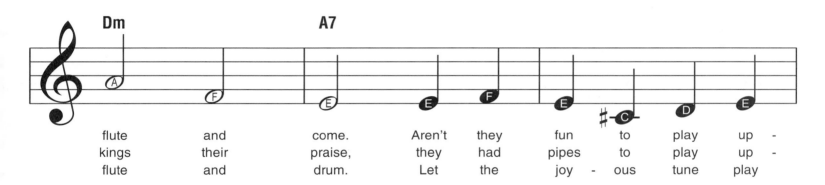

flute and come. Aren't they fun to play up -
kings and their praise, they had fun pipes to play up -
flute and drum. Let the joy - ous tune play

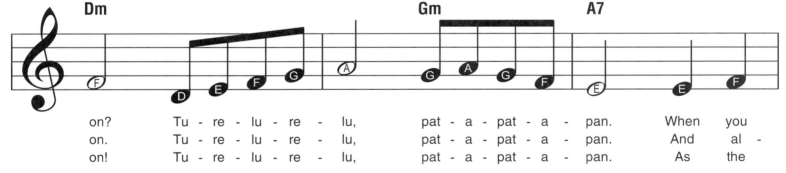

on? Tu - re - lu - re - lu, pat - a - pat - a - pan. When you
on. Tu - re - lu - re - lu, pat - a - pat - a - pan. And al -
on! Tu - re - lu - re - lu, pat - a - pat - a - pan. As the

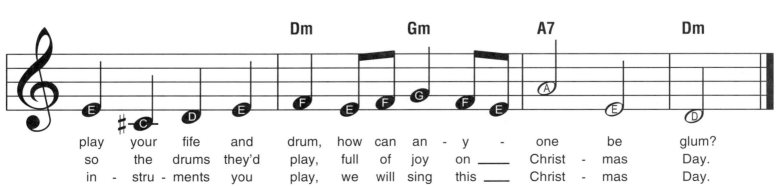

play your fife and drum, how can an - y - one be glum?
so the drums they'd play, full of joy on ____ Christ - mas Day.
in - stru - ments you play, we will sing this ____ Christ - mas Day.

Parade of the Wooden Soldiers

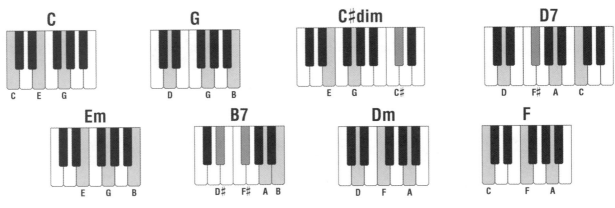

English Lyrics by Ballard MacDonald
Music by Leon Jessel

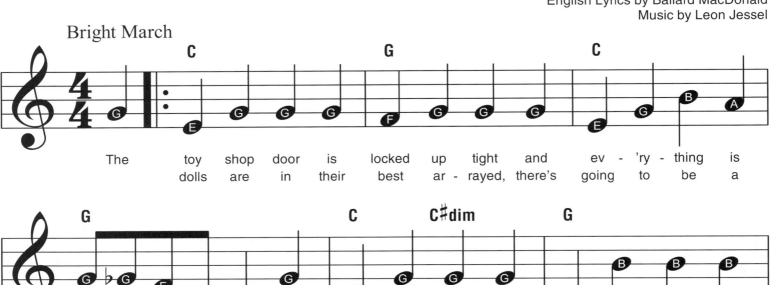

Bright March

The toy shop door is locked up tight and ev - 'ry - thing is
dolls are in their best ar - rayed, there's going to be a

qui - et for the night, when sud - den - ly the clock strikes twelve; the
won - der - ful pa - rade. Hark to the drum, oh! here they come, cries

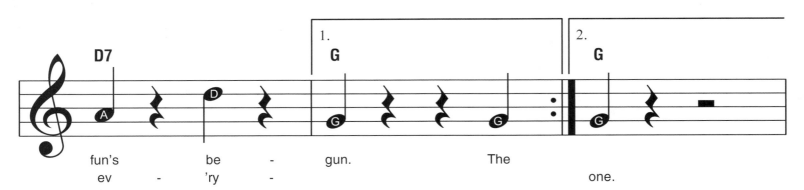

fun's be - gun. The
ev - 'ry - one.

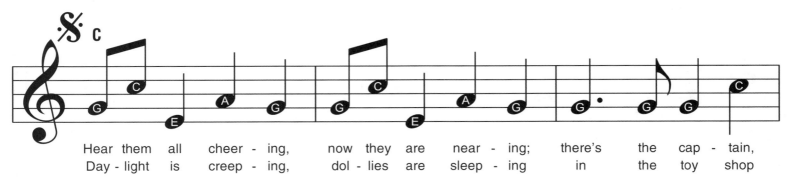

Hear them all cheer - ing, now they are near - ing; there's the cap - tain,
Day - light is creep - ing, dol - lies are sleep - ing in the toy shop

stiff   as   starch.   Bay - o - nets   flash - ing,   mu - sic   is   crash - ing
win - dow   fast.   Sol - diers   so   jol - ly   think   of   each   dol - ly,

as   the   wood - en   sol - diers   march.   Sa - bres   a - clink - ing,   sol - diers   a - wink - ing
dream - ing   of   the   night   that's   past.   When   in   the   morn - ing,   with - out   a   warn - ing,

at   each   pret - ty   lit - tle   maid.   Here   they   come!   Here   they   come!

To Coda

D.S. al Coda
(Return to 𝄋, play to ⊕ and skip to Coda)

Here   they   come!   Here   they   come!   Wood - en   sol - diers   on   pa - rade.

CODA

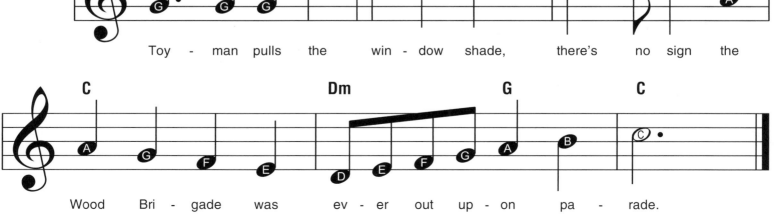

Toy - man   pulls   the   win - dow   shade,   there's   no   sign   the

Wood   Bri - gade   was   ev - er   out   up - on   pa - rade.

Rise Up, Shepherd, and Follow

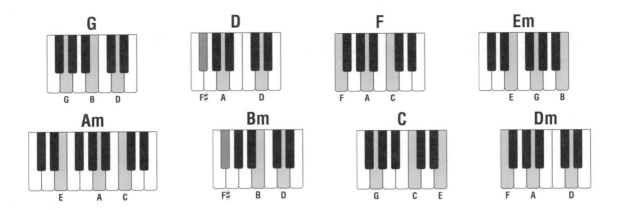

African-American Spiritual

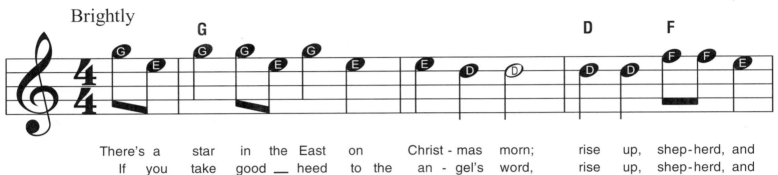

Brightly

There's a   star   in the East   on   Christ - mas   morn;   rise   up,   shep-herd, and
If   you   take   good __ heed   to the   an - gel's   word,   rise   up,   shep-herd, and

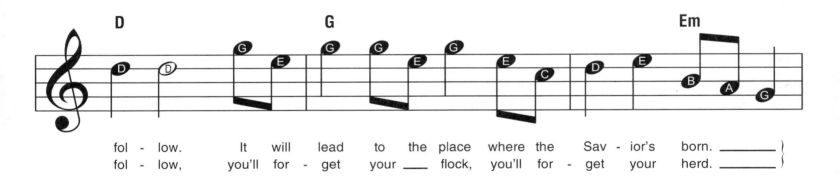

fol - low.   It   will   lead   to   the place   where the   Sav - ior's   born. _____
fol - low,   you'll   for - get   your __ flock,   you'll   for - get   your   herd. _____

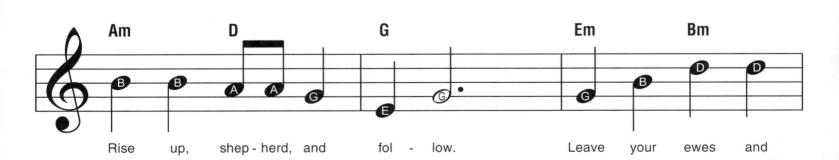

Rise   up,   shep - herd,   and   fol - low.   Leave   your   ewes   and

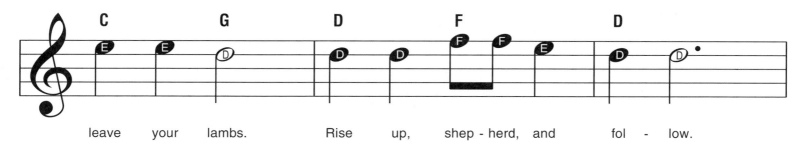

leave your lambs. Rise up, shep - herd, and fol - low.

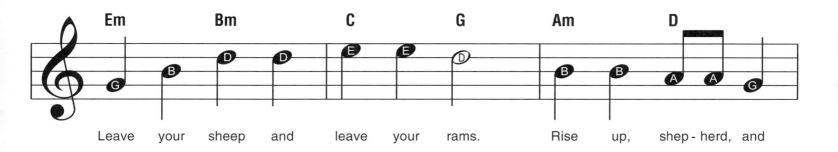

Leave your sheep and leave your rams. Rise up, shep - herd, and

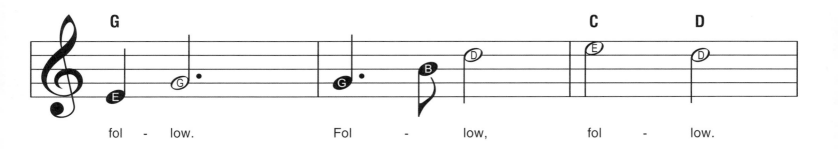

fol - low. Fol - low, fol - low.

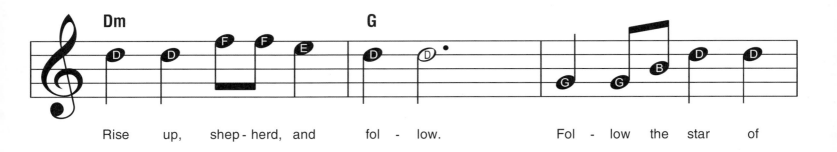

Rise up, shep - herd, and fol - low. Fol - low the star of

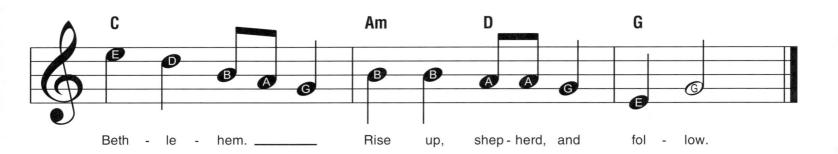

Beth - le - hem. _____ Rise up, shep - herd, and fol - low.

84

Silent Night

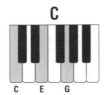 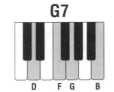 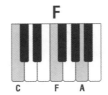

Words by Joseph Mohr
Translated by John F. Young
Music by Franz X. Gruber

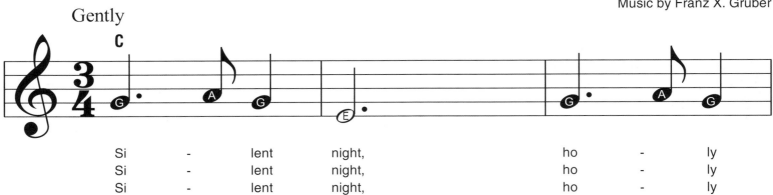

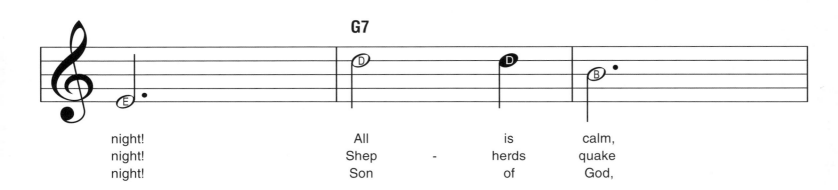

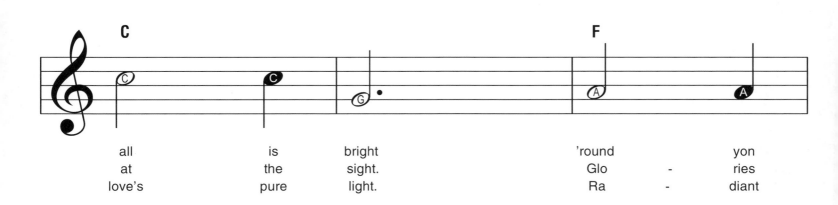

Sing We Now of Christmas

 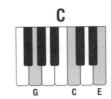 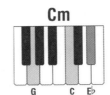 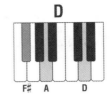

Traditional French Carol

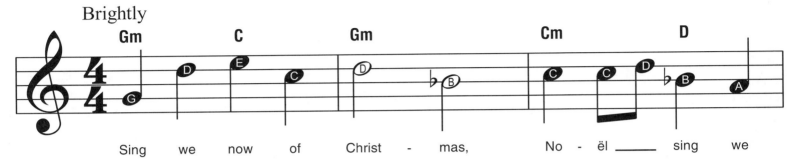

Sing we now of Christ - mas, No - ël ____ sing we

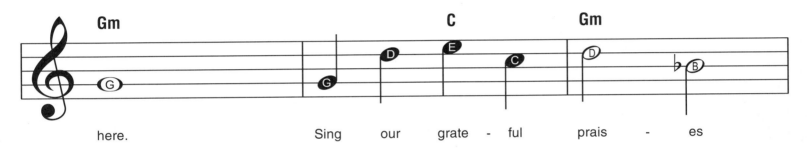

here. Sing our grate - ful prais - es

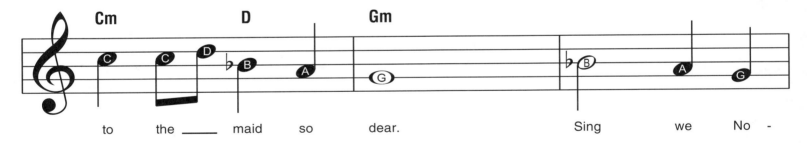

to the ____ maid so dear. Sing we No -

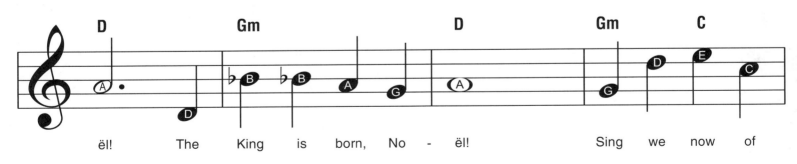

ël! The King is born, No - ël! Sing we now of

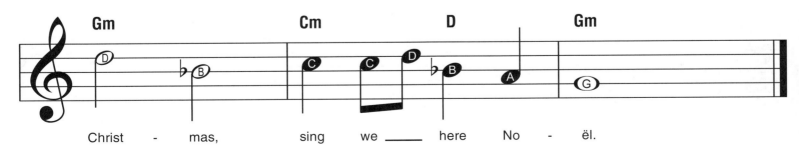

Christ - mas, sing we ____ here No - ël.

Still, Still, Still

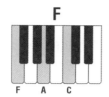
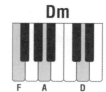
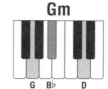
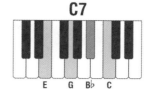

Salzburg Melody, c.1819
Traditional Austrian Text

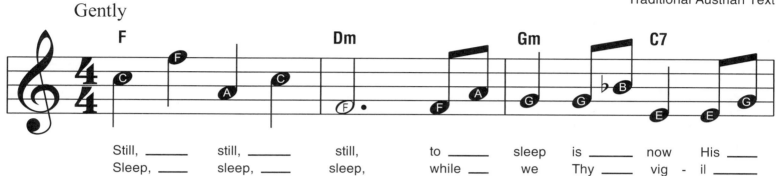

Still, _____ still, _____ still, to _____ sleep is _____ now His _____
Sleep, _____ sleep, _____ sleep, while _____ we Thy _____ vig - il _____

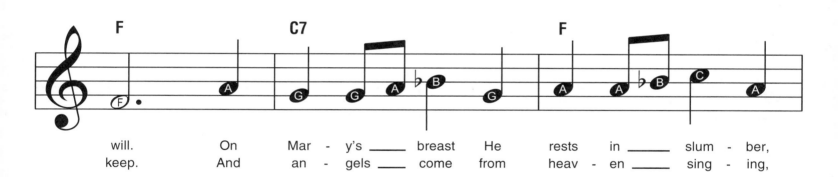

will. On Mar - y's _____ breast He rests in _____ slum - ber,
keep. And an - gels _____ come from heav - en _____ sing - ing,

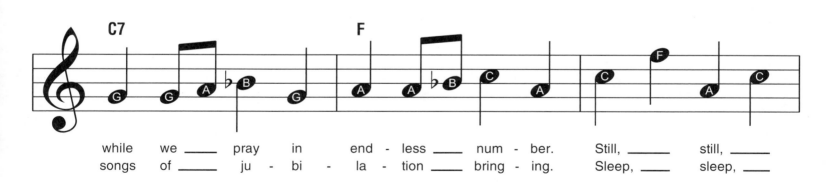

while we _____ pray in end - less _____ num - ber. Still, _____ still, _____
songs of _____ ju - bi - la - tion _____ bring - ing. Sleep, _____ sleep, _____

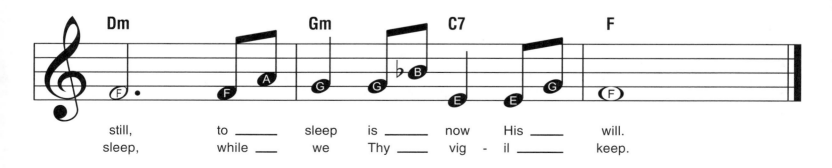

still, to _____ sleep is _____ now His _____ will.
sleep, while _____ we Thy _____ vig - il _____ keep.

Star of the East

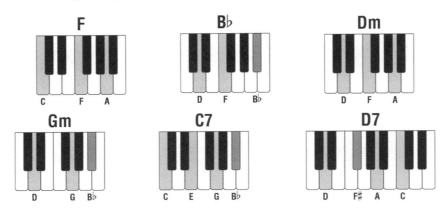

Words by George Cooper
Music by Amanda Kennedy

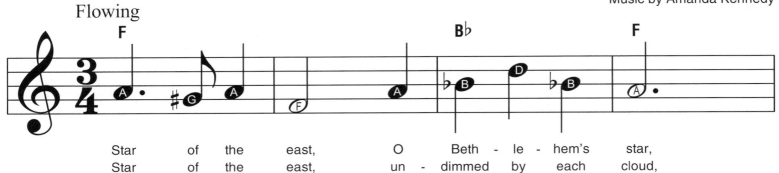

Star of the east, O Beth - le - hem's star,
Star of the east, un - dimmed by each cloud,

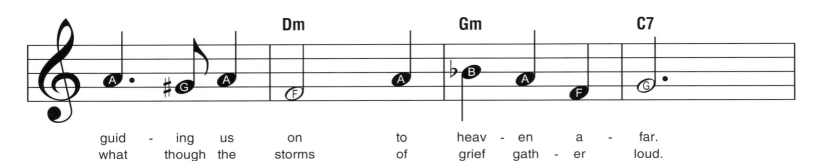

guid - ing us on to heav - en a - far.
what though the storms of grief gath - er loud.

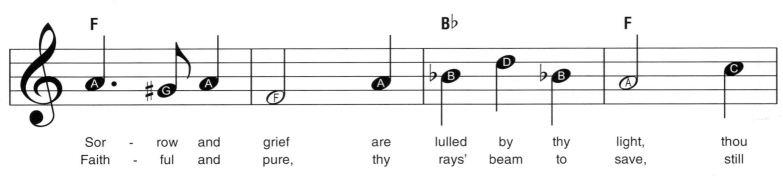

Sor - row and grief are lulled by thy light, thou
Faith - ful and pure, thy rays' beam to save, still

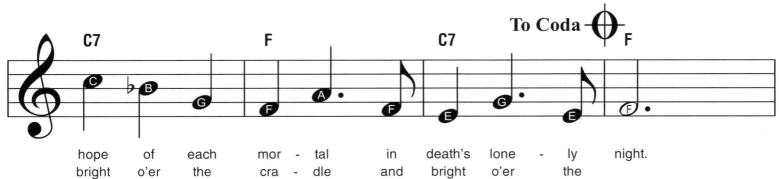

hope of each mor - tal in death's lone - ly night.
bright o'er each the cra - dle and bright o'er the

Sussex Carol

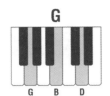 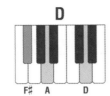 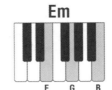 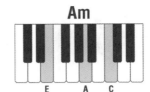 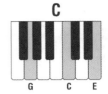

Traditional English Carol

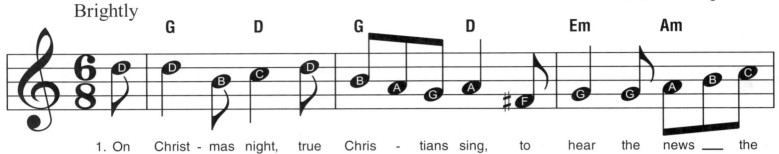

1. On Christ - mas night, true Chris - tians sing, to hear the news __ the
2.–4. *(See additional lyrics)*

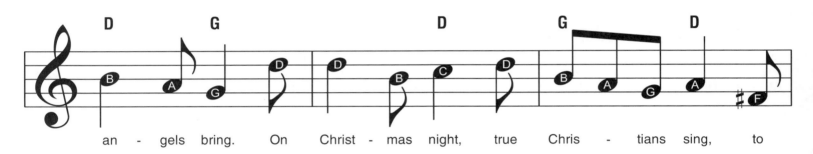

an - gels bring. On Christ - mas night, true Chris - tians sing, to

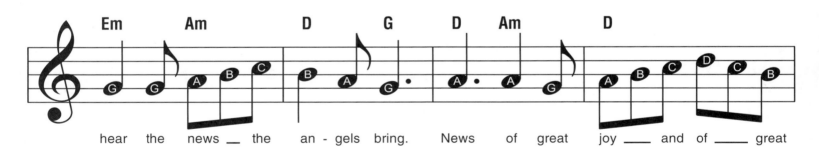

hear the news __ the an - gels bring. News of great joy __ and of __ great

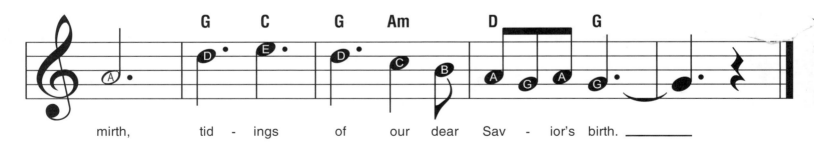

mirth, tid - ings of our dear Sav - ior's birth. _____

Additional Lyrics

2. The King of kings to us is giv'n,
The Lord of earth and King of heav'n.
The King of kings to us is giv'n,
The Lord of earth and King of heav'n.
Angels and men with joy may sing
Of blest Jesus, their Savior King.

3. From out the darkness have we light,
Which makes the angels sing this night.
From out the darkness have we light,
Which makes the angels sing this night.
"Glory to God, His peace to men,
And goodwill evermore, amen."

4. So how on earth can men be sad,
When Jesus comes to make us glad?
So how on earth can men be sad,
When Jesus comes to make us glad?
From all our sins to set us free,
Buying for us our liberty.

Toyland
from BABES IN TOYLAND

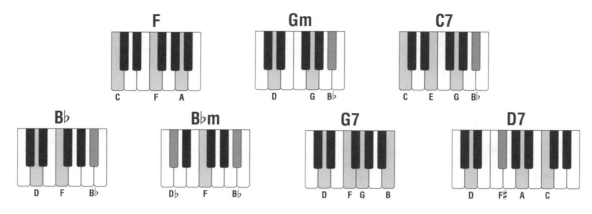

Words by Glen MacDonough
Music by Victor Herbert

Slowly, in 2

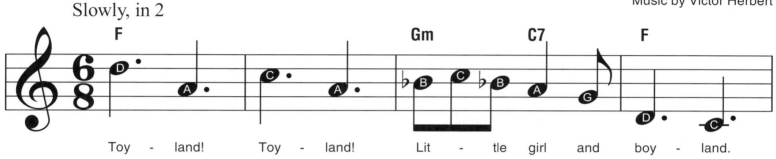

Toy - land! Toy - land! Lit - tle girl and boy - land.

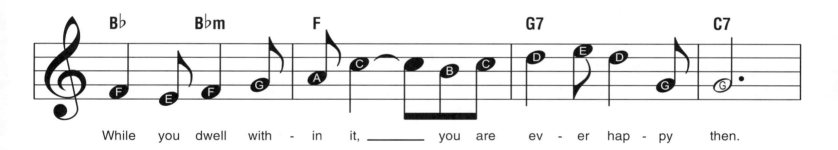

While you dwell with - in it, _____ you are ev - er hap - py then.

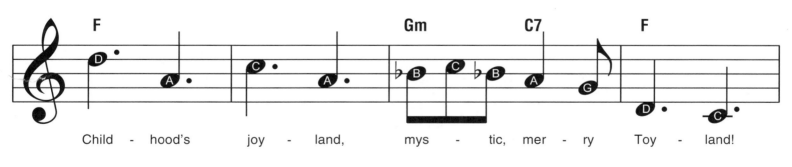

Child - hood's joy - land, mys - tic, mer - ry Toy - land!

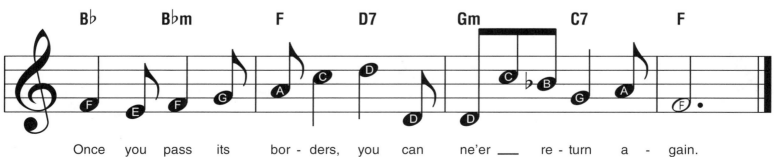

Once you pass its bor - ders, you can ne'er _____ re - turn a - gain.

The Twelve Days of Christmas

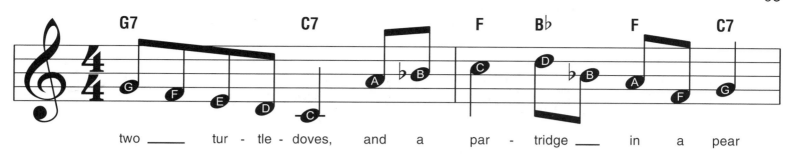

two ___ tur - tle - doves, and a par - tridge ___ in a pear

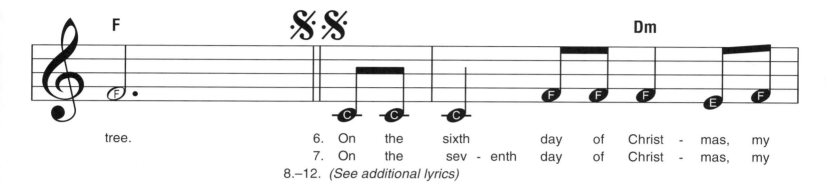

tree.

6. On the sixth day of Christ - mas, my
7. On the sev - enth day of Christ - mas, my
8.–12. *(See additional lyrics)*

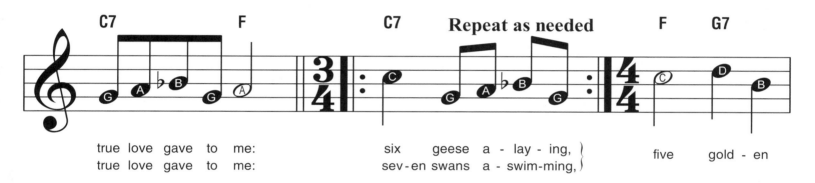

Repeat as needed

true love gave to me: six geese a - lay - ing,
true love gave to me: sev - en swans a - swim-ming,

five gold - en

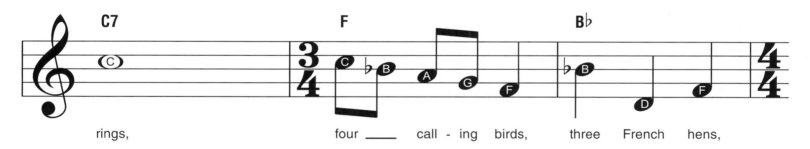

rings, four ___ call - ing birds, three French hens,

(D.S.S. 6x, then Fine)

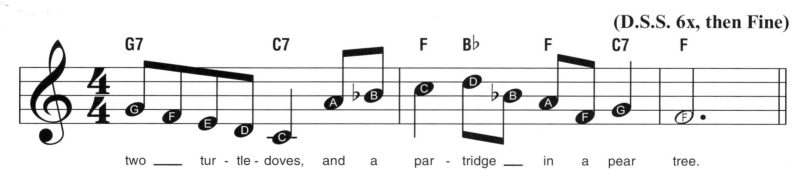

two ___ tur - tle - doves, and a par - tridge ___ in a pear tree.

Additional Lyrics

8. On the eighth day... eight maids a-milking...
9. On the ninth day... nine ladies dancing...
10. On the tenth day... ten lords a-leaping...
11. On the 'leventh day... 'leven pipers piping...
12. On the twelfth day... twelve drummers drumming...

Ukrainian Bell Carol

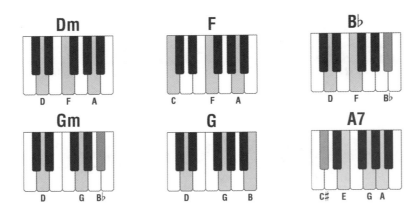

Traditional
Music by Mykola Leontovych

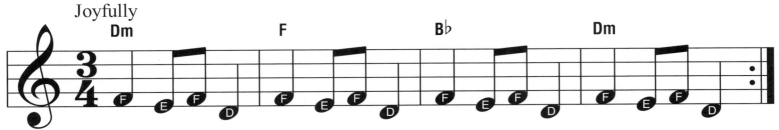

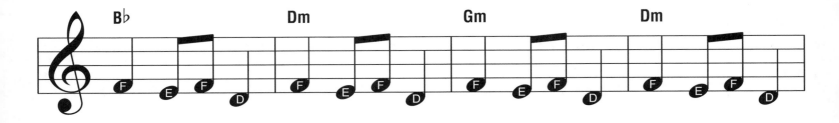

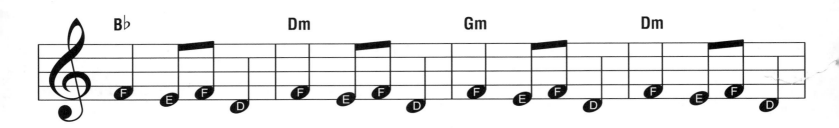

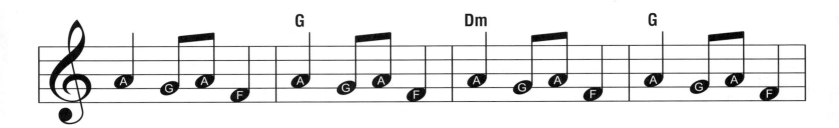

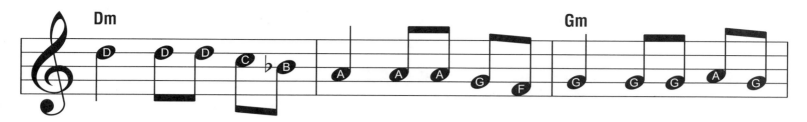

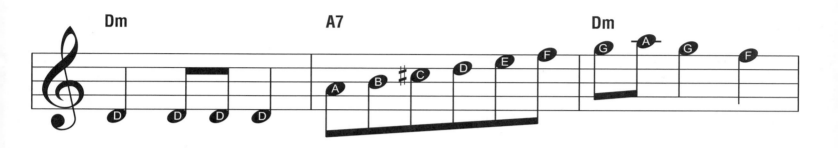

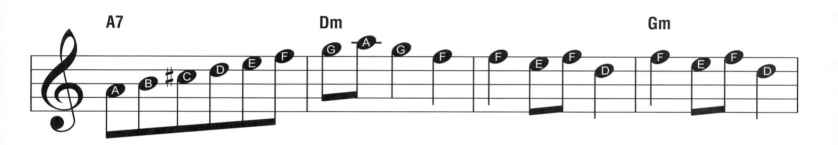

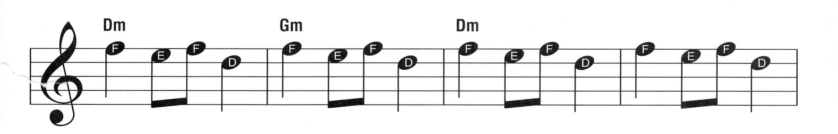

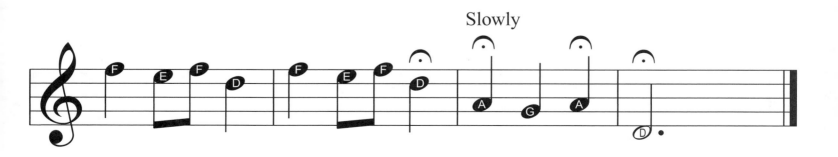

Up on the Housetop

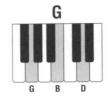 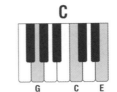 

Words and Music by
B.R. Hanby

We Wish You a Merry Christmas

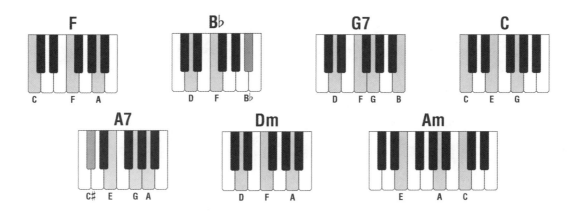

Traditional English Folksong

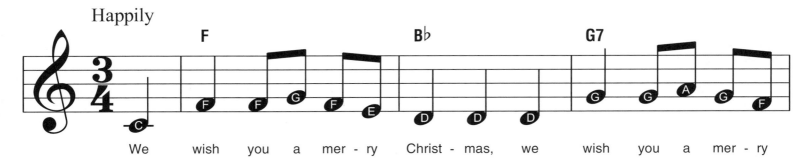

We wish you a mer-ry Christ-mas, we wish you a mer-ry

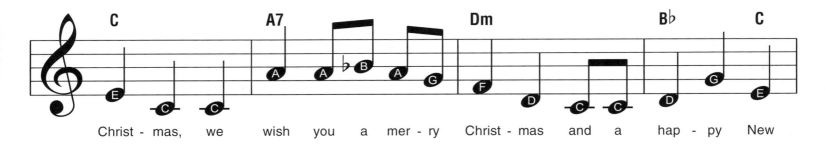

Christ-mas, we wish you a mer-ry Christ-mas and a hap-py New

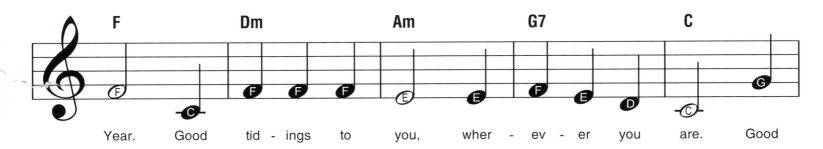

Year. Good tid-ings to you, wher-ev-er you are. Good

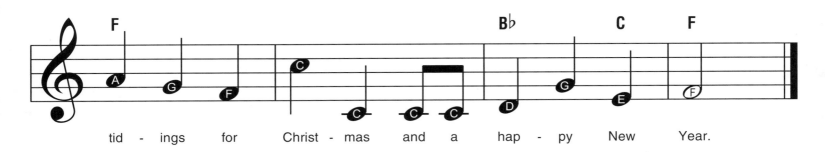

tid-ings for Christ-mas and a hap-py New Year.

We Three Kings of Orient Are

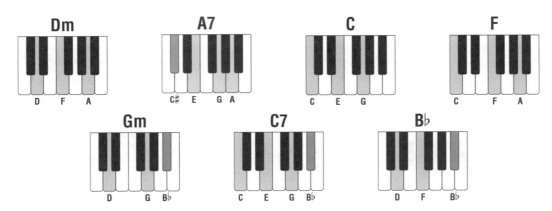

Words and Music by
John H. Hopkins, Jr.

Moderately fast

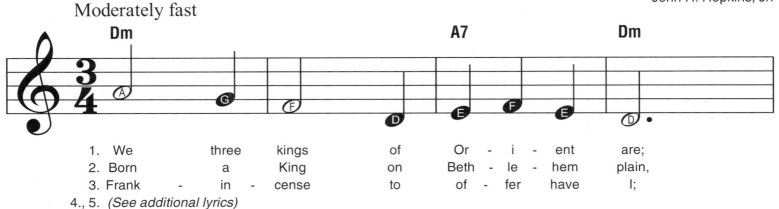

1. We three kings of Or - i - ent are;
2. Born a King on Beth - le - hem plain,
3. Frank - in - cense to of - fer have I;
4., 5. *(See additional lyrics)*

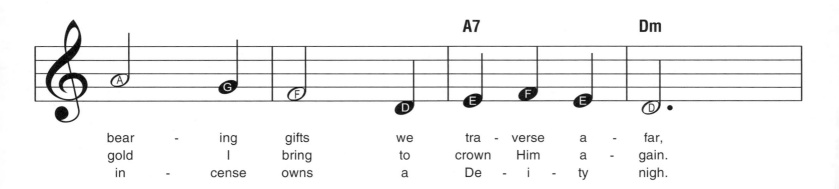

bear - ing gifts we tra - verse a - far,
gold I bring to crown Him a - gain.
in - cense owns a De - i - ty nigh.

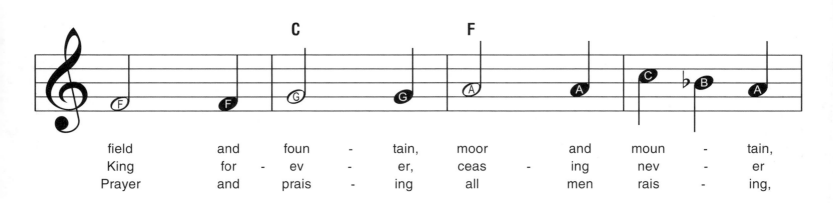

field and foun - tain, moor and moun - tain,
King for - ev - er, ceas - ing nev - er
Prayer and prais - ing all men rais - ing,

Additional Lyrics

4. Myrrh is mine; its bitter perfume
Breathes a life of gathering gloom;
Sorr'wing, sighing, bleeding, dying,
Sealed in the stone-cold tomb.
Refrain

5. Glorious now, behold Him arise,
King and God and sacrifice.
Alleluia, alleluia
Sounds through the earth and skies.
Refrain

What Child Is This?

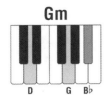

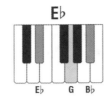
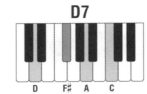
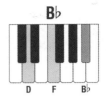

Words by William C. Dix
16th Century English Melody

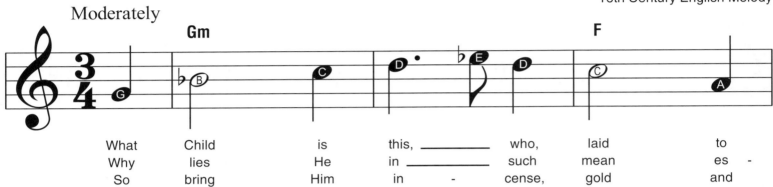

What Child is this, _____ who, laid to
Why lies He in - _____ such mean es -
So bring Him in - cense, gold and

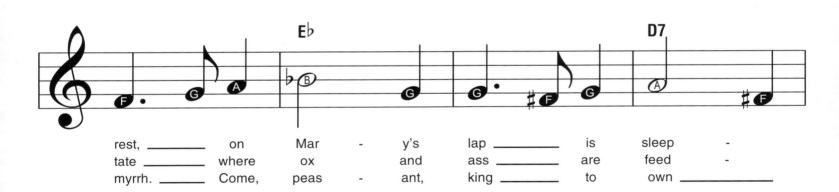

rest, _____ on Mar - y's lap _____ is sleep -
tate _____ where ox and ass _____ are feed -
myrrh. _____ Come, peas - ant, king _____ to own _____

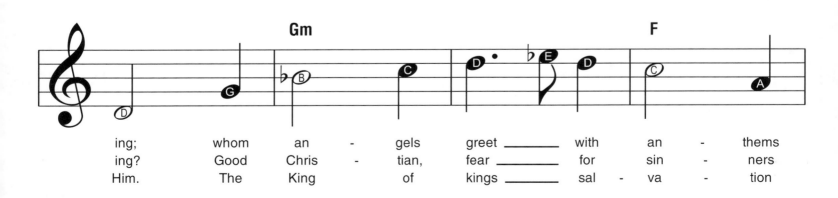

ing; whom an - gels greet _____ with an - thems
ing? Good Chris - tian, fear _____ for sin - ners
Him. The King of kings _____ sal - va - tion

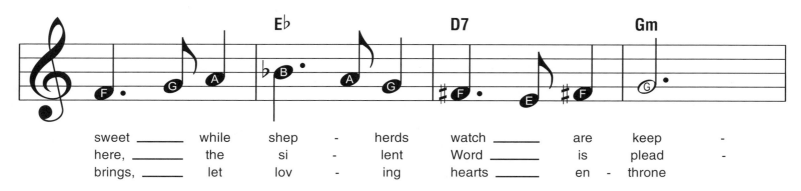

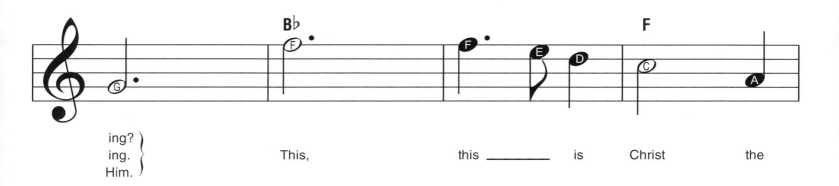

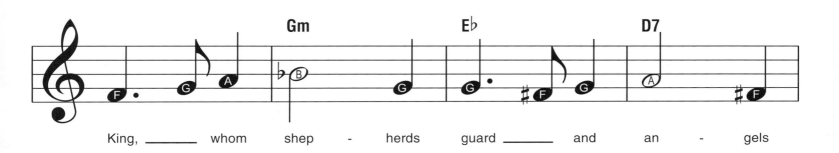

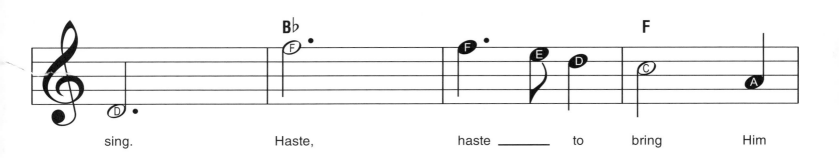

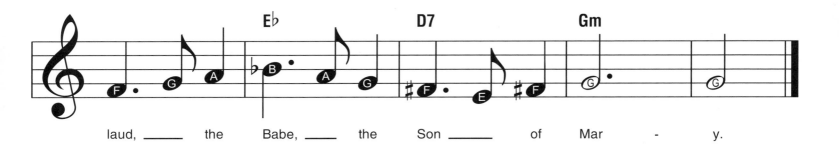

While Shepherds Watched Their Flocks

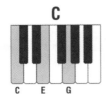
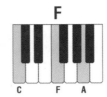
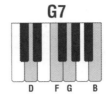

Words by Nahum Tate
Music by George Frideric Handel

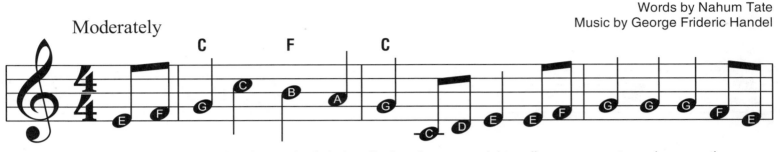

1. While ___ shep-herds watched their flocks by ___ night, all ___ seat-ed on the ___
2. "Fear ___ not!" said he, for might-y ___ dread had ___ seized their trou-bled ___
3.–6. *(See additional lyrics)*

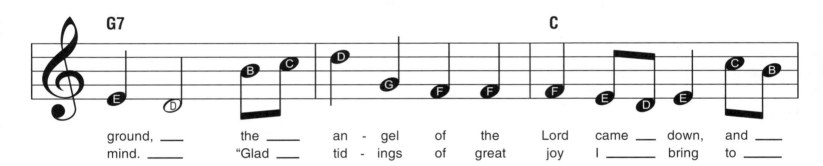

ground, ___ the ___ an-gel of the Lord came ___ down, and ___
mind. ___ "Glad ___ tid-ings of great joy I ___ bring to ___

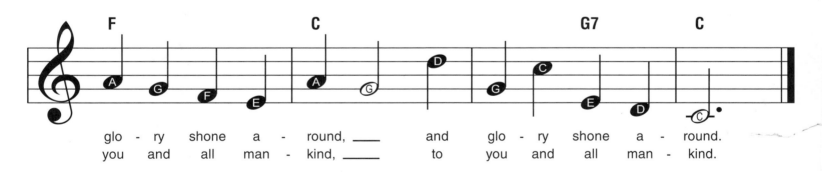

glo-ry shone a-round, ___ and glo-ry shone a-round.
you and all man-kind, ___ to you and all man-kind.

Additional Lyrics

3. To you, in David's town this day,
   Is born of David's line,
   The Savior, who is Christ the Lord;
   And this shall be the sign,
   And this shall be the sign:

4. The heavenly Babe you there shall find
   To human view displayed,
   All meanly wrapped in swathing bands,
   And in a manger laid,
   And in a manger laid."

5. Thus spake the seraph; and forthwith
   Appeared a shining throng
   Of angels praising God on high,
   Who thus addressed their song,
   Who thus addressed their song:

6. "All glory be to God on high,
   And to the earth be peace;
   Good will henceforth from heav'n to men,
   Begin and never cease,
   Begin and never cease!"

It's super easy! This series features accessible arrangements for piano, with simple right-hand melody, letter names inside each note, and basic left-hand chord diagrams. Each volume includes 60 great songs!

KIDS' SONGS

"C" Is for Cookie • Do-Re-Mi • Electricity • Hush, Little Baby • I'm Popeye the Sailor Man • Over the Rainbow • Puff the Magic Dragon • The Rainbow Connection • Sesame Street Theme • Tomorrow • The Wheels on the Bus • You Are My Sunshine • and many more.
00198009...$14.99

ANDREW LLOYD WEBBER

Angel of Music • Any Dream Will Do • Buenos Aires • Close Every Door • Don't Cry for Me Argentina • Gus: the Theatre Cat • Love Never Dies • Memory • The Music of the Night • The Perfect Year • Superstar • Unexpected Song • Wishing You Were Somehow Here Again • You're in the Band • and more.
00249580 ....$14.99

MOVIE SONGS

Chariots of Fire • City of Stars • Eye of the Tiger • Happy • Kiss from a Rose • Moon River • Over the Rainbow • Somewhere Out There • (I've Had) The Time of My Life • What a Wonderful World • and more.
00233670...$14.99

POP STANDARDS

Africa • Bridge over Troubled Water • Careless Whisper • Every Breath You Take • God Only Knows • Hallelujah • Just the Way You Are • Right Here Waiting • Stand by Me • Tears in Heaven • The Wind Beneath My Wings • You've Got a Friend • and many more.
00233770 ....$14.99

THREE CHORD SONGS

All About That Bass • Beat It • Clocks • Daughter • Evil Ways • Folsom Prison Blues • Hound Dog • I Still Haven't Found What I'm Looking For • Jolene • Kiss • La Bamba • The Music of the Night • Old Time Rock & Roll • Riptide • Sweet Caroline • Twist and Shout • Use Somebody • Walk of Life • and more.
00249664 ....$14.99

THE BEATLES

All You Need Is Love • Come Together • Get Back • Here Comes the Sun • Hey Jude • I Want to Hold Your Hand • Let It Be • Something • We Can Work It Out • Yesterday • and many more.
00198161 .... $14.99

BROADWAY

All I Ask of You • Bring Him Home • Cabaret • Dancing Queen • Edelweiss • Footloose • Hello, Dolly! • Memory • Ol' Man River • Seasons of Love • Try to Remember • and many more.
00193871.. $14.99

CHRISTMAS SONGS

All I Want for Christmas Is You • Do You Hear What I Hear • Frosty the Snow Man • Have Yourself a Merry Little Christmas • Mary, Did You Know? • Rudolph the Red-Nosed Reindeer • Silver Bells • White Christmas • Winter Wonderland • and more.
00236850 .... $14.99

CLASSICAL

Canon (Pachelbel) • Für Elise (Beethoven) • Jesu, Joy of Man's Desiring • (J.S. Bach) • Lullaby (Brahms) • On the Beautiful Blue Danube (Strauss) • Pomp and Circumstance (Elgar) • Trumpet Voluntary (Clarke) • William Tell Overture (Rossini) • and many more.
00194693 .... $14.99

DISNEY

Be Our Guest • Chim Chim Cher-ee • A Dream Is a Wish Your Heart Makes • Friend like Me • Heigh-Ho • Kiss the Girl • Let It Go • A Spoonful of Sugar • When You Wish upon a Star • Winnie the Pooh • You've Got a Friend in Me • and more.
00199558 .... $14.99

HIT SONGS

All of Me • Brave • Can't Feel My Face • Ex's & Oh's • Ho Hey • Jar of Hearts • Lost Boy • Riptide • Rolling in the Deep • Shake It Off • Stay with Me • A Thousand Years • and more.
00194367 .... $14.99

HYMNS

All Creatures of Our God and King • Amazing Grace • Be Thou My Vision • Crown Him with Many Crowns • For the Beauty of the Earth • I Love to Tell the Story • O Worship the King • Rock of Ages • We Gather Together • What a Friend We Have in Jesus • and many more.
00194659..$14.99

JAZZ STANDARDS

Body and Soul • Cheek to Cheek • Embraceable You • Georgia on My Mind • I Got Rhythm • The Nearness of You • Satin Doll • Someone to Watch over Me • The Way You Look Tonight • and more.
00233687..$14.99

HAL•LEONARD®
WWW.HALLEONARD.COM

HAL LEONARD PRESENTS
FAKE BOOKS FOR BEGINNERS!

Entry-level fake books! These books feature larger-than-most fake book notation with simplified harmonies and melodies – and all songs are in the key of C. An introduction addresses basic instruction in playing from a fake book.

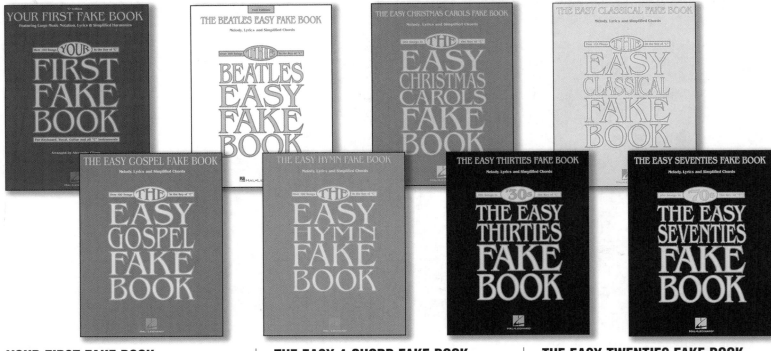

YOUR FIRST FAKE BOOK
00240112......................$20.50

THE EASY FAKE BOOK
00240144......................$19.99

THE SIMPLIFIED FAKE BOOK
00240168......................$19.95

**THE BEATLES EASY
FAKE BOOK – 2ND EDITION**
00171200......................$25.00

THE EASY CHILDREN'S FAKE BOOK
00240428 ....$19.99

THE EASY CHRISTIAN FAKE BOOK
00240328......................$19.99

**THE EASY CHRISTMAS CAROLS
FAKE BOOK**
00238187 ....$19.99

THE EASY CLASSIC ROCK FAKE BOOK
00240389 ....$19.99

THE EASY CLASSICAL FAKE BOOK
00240262......................$19.99

THE EASY COUNTRY FAKE BOOK
00240319......................$19.99

THE EASY DISNEY FAKE BOOK
00240551......................$19.99

THE EASY FOLKSONG FAKE BOOK
00240360......................$19.99

THE EASY 4-CHORD FAKE BOOK
00118752 ....$19.99

THE EASY G MAJOR FAKE BOOK
00142279 ....$19.99

THE EASY GOSPEL FAKE BOOK
00240169......................$19.99

THE EASY HYMN FAKE BOOK
00240207......................$19.99

**THE EASY JAZZ STANDARDS
FAKE BOOK**
00102346......................$19.99

THE EASY LATIN FAKE BOOK
00240333......................$19.99

THE EASY LOVE SONGS FAKE BOOK
00159775 ....$19.99

THE EASY MOVIE FAKE BOOK
00240295......................$19.95

THE EASY POP/ROCK FAKE BOOK
00141667 ....$19.99

THE EASY 3-CHORD FAKE BOOK
00240388 ....$19.99

THE EASY WORSHIP FAKE BOOK
00240265......................$19.99

**MORE OF THE EASY WORSHIP
FAKE BOOK**
00240362 ....$19.99

THE EASY TWENTIES FAKE BOOK
00240336 ....$19.99

THE EASY THIRTIES FAKE BOOK
00240335 ....$19.99

THE EASY FORTIES FAKE BOOK
00240252......................$19.99

THE EASY FIFTIES FAKE BOOK
00240255......................$19.95

THE EASY SIXTIES FAKE BOOK
00240253......................$19.99

THE EASY SEVENTIES FAKE BOOK
00240256......................$19.95

THE EASY EIGHTIES FAKE BOOK
00240340 ....$19.99

THE EASY NINETIES FAKE BOOK
00240341 ....$19.99

HAL•LEONARD®

www.halleonard.com

*Prices, contents and availability
subject to change without notice.*

0518